Reverse the Search

Reverse THE Search

How to Turn Job Seeking into Job Shopping

Madeline Mann

PORTFOLIO | PENGUIN

Portfolio/Penguin
An imprint of Penguin Random House LLC
1745 Broadway, New York, NY 10019
penguinrandomhouse.com

Most Portfolio books are available at a discount when purchased in quantity for sales promotions or corporate use. Special editions, which include personalized covers, excerpts, and corporate imprints, can be created when purchased in large quantities. For more information, please call (212) 572-2232 or e-mail specialmarkets@penguinrandomhouse.com. Your local bookstore can also assist with discounted bulk purchases using the Penguin Random House corporate Business-to-Business program. For assistance in locating a participating retailer, e-mail B2B@penguinrandomhouse.com.

BOOK DESIGN AND ILLUSTRATIONS BY TANYA MAIBORODA

Library of Congress Cataloging-in-Publication Data

Names: Mann, Madeline, author.
Title: Reverse the search: how to turn job seeking into job shopping / Madeline Mann.
Description: New York: Portfolio/Penguin, [2025] | Includes bibliographical references and index.
Identifiers: LCCN 2024031254 (print) | LCCN 2024031255 (ebook) | ISBN 9780593717660 (hardcover) | ISBN 9780593717677 (ebook)
Subjects: LCSH: Job hunting.
Classification: LCC HF5382.7 .M3555 2025 (print) | LCC HF5382.7 (ebook) | DDC 650.14—dc23/eng/20240719
LC record available at https://lccn.loc.gov/2024031254
LC ebook record available at https://lccn.loc.gov/2024031255

Printed in the United States of America
1   3   5   7   9   10   8   6   4   2

The authorized representative in the EU for product safety and compliance is Penguin Random House Ireland, Morrison Chambers, 32 Nassau Street, Dublin D02 YH68, Ireland, https://eu-contact.penguin.ie.

To my husband, Henry.
Your steadfast support means everything.

Contents

Introduction

When I was leading the human resources department at a growth-stage technology company, somewhere around the thousandth job application I reviewed, it dawned on me that most job seekers need some serious help with the way they present themselves in the job search. While some unlikely candidates blew the hiring team out of the water, compelling us to hire them, many perfectly qualified candidates struggled to barely get past the first interview. Like a DIY psychology researcher, I started to track my own data points, and I began to see clear patterns of what led job seekers to repeated success, or guaranteed failure.

Feeling it was wrong to keep these insights to myself when so many people needed the help, I did what I thought would make me a hero to job seekers: I replied to their applications with feedback. After spending a couple hours crafting feedback emails to nearly a hundred candidates, I sat back with the satisfied feeling of a job well done, and waited for the thank-yous to come pouring in.

What actually happened? They *hated* me.

Here are a few of the (many) negative responses I got:

- "Well you're never hearing from me again. You obviously don't appreciate talent."
- "lol. you're a joke."
- "Frankly you have no expertise to understand my skill set, I'd like to talk to someone else in the company."

And if the response wasn't negative, it was a barrage of more questions. More emails. I was drowning in so many threads that it took too much time and energy to keep up. The more responses I sent, the more I regretted saying anything at all.

I clearly needed to take a different approach. My next strategy, I decided, would be to call every candidate who interviewed with the company and deliver the rejection over the phone, providing feedback if they wanted it. This, I was sure, was the most considerate and helpful thing I could do for these candidates who had dedicated their time to the process. My coworkers caught wind of my new approach and told me I was out of my mind. "People don't want to be rejected over the phone," they insisted. So I sent out a survey to the whole company, which read:

Would you prefer to be rejected for a job via phone or via email with an option to hop on a call?

Overwhelmingly, 82 percent of employees voted "email," with the remaining 18 percent preferring a phone call. It turns out that being rejected on the phone is a vulnerable and awkward situation. Most people would rather not get their hopes up or have to accept bad news in real time.

Having struck out twice now, I was at a loss as to what I should do. I finally turned to a mentor of mine, and he said that I needed to reach people *before* a rejection, and only people who were open to feedback (and most people, he stated, are not). So I looked online to see what resources were out there for job seekers. The results were disappointing. Endless articles and videos regurgitated outdated advice while boring viewers to tears. Tips like "Be confident" and "Network" left so many people feeling confused and helpless. So I set out to create videos online that were highly specific, modern, and a bit cheeky, to finally get job seekers real results.

I started putting out videos with behind-the-scenes secrets to ace the job search and gain promotions under the handle "Self Made Millennial," which I chose as a title that reflected the aspirations of the viewer (but the brand has since expanded to other generations). The beginning was humble. I woke up several hours before work each morning to focus on the channel and continued to grind on it each evening. I didn't have the deep pockets to outsource any of it, so I became a one-woman shop of script writing, graphic design, description writing, social-media promotion, and video editing. I invested thousands of hours and dollars into creating the content and paying for the equipment and software needed. And after one year, what incredible results did I have to show for it?

A couple of hundred views per video, with a lucky few cracking a thousand.

I felt like a failure. I had expected much bigger things.

But the spark that kept me going was the small trickle of positive feedback I was receiving; at that point, I had gotten dozens of comments from people who did manage to find my content, saying that it was the best content they had seen on the topic and wondering, "Why doesn't this video have more views? You are so underrated!" The comments gave me the hope I needed to keep going, and fueled my ambition to further my reach and help more people. Then, suddenly, I was laid off from my job.

I was crushed. I loved my job, and to have it ripped away suddenly one day was completely destabilizing. While I knew I eventually wanted to get back to a human resources role, I also knew that this was an opportunity to completely change my approach to the videos with my extra free time outside of job searching. So I forked over a five-figure sum to invest in coaching to get the channel off of the ground. I felt slightly reckless doing this when I had no income and had to split up the payment on multiple credit cards, but I had a vision.

The investment paid off! Word got out that people were having incredible success implementing the advice from my content, and the viewership grew from thousands to millions. Opportunities started flowing in at a rapid rate to appear on top news networks, speak at conferences, interview for incredible jobs, and collaborate with some of the most recognizable companies in the world. Funnily enough, my journey mirrors that of job seekers: it's one thing to have all the right skills, but having an excellent strategy to get noticed is what unlocks incredible opportunity.

In the meantime, though, I had started a new job in human resources, and continued loving my career, landing a series of back-to-back dream jobs. I never thought anything could tear me away from my human resources role. But eventually, my career coaching became so in demand, and the success stories were so staggering, that I ultimately left my full-time job—on my own terms this time!—to serve a higher purpose of helping job seekers everywhere. I tell you this because I am someone who *loved* working a full-time job. I wasn't running *from* the corporate world, but running *to* a calling that helped me assist others in finding the same fulfillment I did.

Every year I receive thousands of emails and comments from professionals whose lives have completely transformed due to learning how to play the job search game and win it. Now, after millions of people reached and thousands of people coached, I've put the key insights that I wish all professionals had from the start of their careers into this book. This is not just the basics on how to get a job for those starting out in their field, though this book will of course be useful to new professionals. While my clients repeatedly say they wish they had known this all so much sooner, the insights in this book can act as a revelation even for folks who have been working for decades.

Having a full-time job can be highly satisfying. It can provide you a great living, allow you a flexible lifestyle, and keep your stress levels low. Yet for many people, this feels impossible. But, as my career demonstrated, it's possible to land that great job. And it's not just luck; it's following a highly specific but easily learnable process called Job Shopping.

Job Shopping is flipping the dynamic of your job search to get companies competing for you. Job Shoppers focus their job search strategy on a specific type of opportunity and then make themselves irresistible to companies hiring for that role. This allows them to attract opportunities, land more offers, and even have companies create roles for them. The whole Job Shopping approach unlocks the power job seekers have (even in the toughest job markets and for "unconventional" candidates) to be the most desirable candidate and have their pick of offers.

JOB SEEKER	JOB SHOPPER
Has unclear goals	Knows exactly what they want
Feels busy and exhausted in job search	Feels focused and in control in job search
Continues to buy more degrees and certifications	Finds ways to demonstrate their skill set
Thinks applying more will land a job faster	Skips online applications for faster ways to get noticed
Stays generic to not "miss out" on different jobs	Positions themselves exactly as what their target companies are looking for
Views interviews as a time to convince the company of their skills	Views interviews as a time to discuss and collaborate with a potential employer
Focuses on the most impressive aspects of their past	Speaks to the needs of the company
Leaves a good impression on the interviewer	Leaves the interviewer seeing them in a league of their own
Eventually lands a job offer	Lands several offers, and has companies competing for them

There are two major barriers standing in the way for professionals when it comes to taking the leap of faith and fully embracing Job Shopping. First, it's recognizing that there is a need for change. We tend to talk ourselves into staying at a job that we don't like. It's the devil we know. It's like walking around with a pebble in your shoe, and instead of stopping to remove it, you try to ignore and adjust to the discomfort.

The second barrier is knowing where to start. We resort back to the easy things we know—fiddle with our résumé, send out applications, wait, eventually land an interview, end up with a single offer, take it, end up not liking it, and within six months are dreaming of being somewhere else.

We don't know how to break this cycle, so a lot of times it leads to inaction. Why put yourself through all the torture of a job search if you're going to end up at a job that doesn't serenade your sensibilities more than your current job? So you stay frozen, or simply go through the motions of a job search.

If you're looking for a reason to *not* take action, you'll find it every time:

- "All the jobs I'm interested in get too many applications."
- "I am just going to get filtered out by their software."
- "Even if I land the interview, they'll just end up rejecting me because of my age/race/gender/other thing outside of my control."
- "I don't really know what I want."

But what if this time, your job search is different?

What if you invest up front in becoming a Job Shopper, and then this job search and all future ones are easier?

What if you present yourself in a way that has companies seeking *you* out to interview?

What if you land an incredible job that sets your career on a great trajectory?

What if your next role allows you exactly the flexibility, finances, and freedom to live your life the way you want?

This isn't pie-in-the-sky thinking, this is completely reasonable thinking. You can have this. It's going to be work, and it's not always going to be fun, but imagine living the exact life you want. It's worth it for that.

So how do you start your transformation into a Job Shopper? In this book you'll get the step-by-step strategy. This is a get-out-your-notebook, dive-into-the-depths-of-your-background, snap-into-action read. The chapters contain "do the work" exercises, and my recommendation is to, in fact, do the work. It's so easy to breeze through the pages, question if this would actually work for your unique situation (gentle reminder: everyone thinks their situation is unique), or pick and choose only the actions that feel most comfy for you to try. Nope.

There's one thing every highly successful Job Shopper I've coached has in common: They go all in on Job Shopping and put the ownership on themselves. They don't blame companies for having "broken interview processes," they don't blame their job, they don't blame their circumstances. They make it happen because they see no other choice. It's time for you to claim it at this moment: you are destined to be a Job Shopper!

The refrain I hear over and over again about the strategies

in this book, from people at all stages of their careers, is "I wish I had known this all sooner."

So many people lament the lost opportunities and the life they could have had once they realize there was a better way all along to get that great job. I once had a coaching client who let me know at the beginning of the session that she was waiting to hear back from a company on its decision about an offer. Several minutes into the session she started shutting down and getting combative. I told her that I noticed her resistance to the coaching and asked her how she was feeling. She vulnerably shared, "This coaching has made me realize that I'm not getting that job offer I'm waiting on."

While it's hard to not feel regret about potential lost opportunities, you've found your way to this book for a reason. The only thing to do now is to look to the future with a new approach. It's never too late to become a Job Shopper.

This book is not just a collection of job search tips; it's a well-honed blueprint of exactly how to execute a strategic job search—and attract opportunities for the rest of your career. I've noticed throughout my coaching career that most people conduct a job search like they've been handed a Rubik's Cube for the first time. They begin rotating the rows, getting a bit hopeful when one side starts to collect similar colors, but consistently end up feeling defeated as their time and effort don't end up leading to a solved cube. A Job Shopper, on the other hand, understands the correct pattern of moves needed to solve a Rubik's Cube, and has practiced enough times that they can solve it swiftly. You don't have to be a genius to solve a Rubik's Cube, you just need to know the strategy. And this book provides the strategies you need, the right twists to the cube, that will finally allow you to feel like the job search isn't so tough after all.

In this book, I'll spend a few chapters deprogramming you of all the unhelpful perspectives and habits you might have learned about job searching in the past. If you're anything like me, you need to know not just *how* to do something but *why*, so you'll get the *why*, as in, why I give the advice I give, and why it actually works, up top.

Then the work begins. You'll start uncovering what your next career move is. This may be quick for you—you pretty much already know what you want and are simply using the strategies in this book to further cement your confidence in that next career move. But even if you're completely unsure exactly what you want next in your career, this book will help you figure it out.

You might be asking yourself if you want to transition to something similar to what you were doing before, or something quite different. Rest assured, this lack of clarity is completely normal, and you'll work toward gaining clarity in the early chapters.

Then you'll start to get in the mindset of an employer. It's like the old movie trope where a woman meets someone who looks like her twin and they switch places and learn a heartfelt lesson of seeing the world from a different perspective. Though, instead of becoming a princess, you'll become an overworked manager who is in the mindset of hiring as quickly as possible. You'll focus on completely changing the way you talk about yourself on your résumé, in interviews, and beyond to appeal to the mind of the employer.

Next, we'll tackle the GLORY Formula, which is designed to help you write the best résumé of your life, but also ends up supercharging your confidence and transforming the way you explain your experiences, in all contexts.

Once you've got the GLORY Formula down solid, you'll dive into how to land job interviews faster than applying online. This includes a passive approach, where companies are finding you and asking you to interview, and an active approach, where you are meeting companies in a way that gets them to notice you. These strategies take concepts like online personal branding optimization and networking and make them systematic and completely doable. The feedback I constantly get from clients is that landing interviews becomes so much easier once the steps are tangible.

The book rounds out with several chapters on acing the interview and negotiating your highest offer. The interview strategies shared are ones that 95 percent of your competition aren't doing, including the Consultative Approach, the Story Toolbox, and Show-Don't-Tell projects. These are approaches that are proven to give you that photo finish as you snag the first-place job offer. The negotiation chapter alone is worth tens of thousands of dollars, as it walks you through how to talk about money from the very first moment you meet a company, until the final moments before signing on the dotted line. After reading and reviewing those steps and scripts, you'll never fumble a salary negotiation again.

We will conclude with a chapter on how to succeed in your next role. The approach of being a Job Shopper is not one that stops once you land the offer. We will discuss the low-effort strategies that will keep you from ever having a fire drill of a job search, and instead have opportunities coming to you passively and comfortably throughout your career. There's still active work you must do, but the ounce of prevention is better than the pound of cure. I never want you to be in a situation where you're panicking to find a job, and with the Career Security that comes from being a Job Shopper, you won't be.

So what's the end result after dedicating yourself to becoming a Job Shopper? You'll have a career that fulfills you and pays you what you're worth. A job that energizes you, and also gives you the space and finances in your life to enjoy your hobbies or spending time with loved ones. A lifetime of exciting opportunities that you get to choose from, without ever feeling like you need to take a job by default.

And the great news is that I'll be with you each step of the way. I'm here to give you the strategies needed to be successful and happy in a career. So get in, reader, we're going Job Shopping.

Reverse the Search

Chapter 1

THE FIVE MYTHS OF JOB SEEKING

Growing up, I mastered the game of academia. School taught me that the way you win is to read the rubric, hit every standard, and turn the assignment in on time, and you'll get your (likely high) grade back by a certain date. So that's what I did. I knew what school expected from me, and I did it.

Applying for colleges was similar. I had a general idea of which colleges I was more or less likely to get into, I filled out the applications, and I heard back from each one within a set timeline.

However, once I entered the corporate world, I realized that all the habits and expectations I had built in academia were as misplaced as a polar bear in the Sahara.

This caused me to struggle in the job search, and even get poor performance reviews at my first corporate job because I was so used to operating under a predictable rubric.

I went from being an A+ student to a C− employee.

Job seeking can feel like such a nebulous process, especially after the clearly defined rules of school. It's time to unlearn the habits we have built, and start seeing the job search process through the employer's eyes. For years, I have heard job seekers state the same false assumptions over and over again about the hiring process. Working in human resources, I know these beliefs to be patently false and damaging to those who hold them.

In this chapter, you'll learn the five myths of job seeking that are likely keeping you stuck—and how you can start to shift your thinking.

Myth 1: "It will be easier if I aim lower."

It is a tremendous misconception that if you are not seeing traction in your job search that you should aim for a job that is at a lower level. You think, "Heck, they've got to want me, as I am super qualified for this role. This will be easy!" and then you get even fewer interviews than before.

Landing a position lower than your level is very challenging to do. That's because companies are more afraid of hiring someone overqualified than they are of hiring someone who doesn't quite have all the qualifications but could learn on the job. They don't see it as a plus to have someone with extra experience. They are looking for someone to do *this* job, not for someone to "get their foot in the door" and then ask for a promotion or salary increase within months of joining. Hiring takes an incredible amount of time and money, starting in the interview process and extending to new employee onboarding. Depending on the type of role, there are estimates that it may take an employee six to twelve months to be fully productive. With that in mind, it's easy to see why the company does not want to hire someone who is treating their role like a placeholder until the *actual* job they want comes along and they leave the company. Unfortunately, overqualified candidates frequently prove this stereotype right, so most companies don't want to take the risk.

This also is the case for people switching careers. For example, if you were manager level in your past job, you might think that, if you are changing careers, you should aim for entry level roles because you don't have manager level experience in this field. But from an employer's perspective, while you are new to the field, that doesn't make you entry level. Entry level candidates are often seen as career newborns,

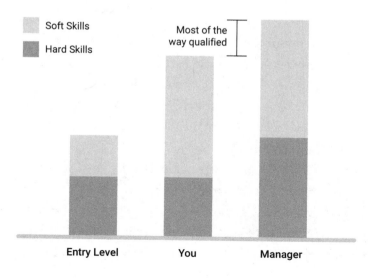

and, as a manager, you actually have a sizable amount of transferable skills that makes a hiring manager not want to put you in an entry level role out of fear that you will get restless.

So while you may think you're giving yourself a leg up by applying for a job you're overqualified for, hiring managers instead see this as you gunning for a higher role or salary increase in the near future, or they think that you'll leave the job as soon as an offer closer to your level slides across your inbox. So instead they'll extend an offer to someone who meets 70 percent of the qualifications but who brings a unique combination of skills from previous jobs and is enthusiastic to learn in the role. Many leaders have learned the hard way that it's easier to train skills than motivate an unchallenged employee.

Myth 2: "I need to get another degree or certification to stand out."

I have *never* seen a hiring manager make a final candidate decision based on degrees and certifications. The thing about formal education is that it's a "check the box" qualification. If a company values and expects a certain degree or certification, it is likely a baseline qualification that most of your competition will have as well.

Now, I won't tell you to skip buying a degree if your dream is being a brain surgeon or the next Judge Judy. Even I wouldn't trust a self-taught surgeon. And I also am not going to deny the allure of having a certain pedigree on your résumé. Some consulting firms, for instance, tend to recruit predominantly from certain MBA programs. In those cases, having that brand-name degree matters. But for the vast majority of jobs out there, doing anything beyond the minimum education qualifications will not help you to stand out.

Furthermore, according to the National Center for Education Statistics, the average master's degree in business administration costs $56,850 in the United States, and a prestigious business school like Harvard Business School will charge you $231,276 for just two years of education.[*] Price tags like that have me thinking there has got to be a more efficient way to level up in your career.

Unfortunately, getting another degree is often the first step professionals think of when they want to make a career move. Take for example my client Gail. When I met Gail, she was fifty-nine years old and had spent her career in accounting. She wanted to transition into a new field but was worried people would focus on her age as a reason to *not* hire her.

Gail's first instinct was to beef up on certifications. She asked if it would be best to get a certification in Tableau or earn her CPA license. My answer? Neither! Getting more education can be a fancy way of procrastinating, like deciding to clean out your closet instead of dealing with your life. Uncovering your next career move and taking unconventional steps to land job offers is more complex than paying for a certification and taking a test. But it takes far less time and money to do so.

---

[*] Melanie Hanson, "Average Cost of a Master's Degree," Education Data Initiative, February 27, 2024, educationdata.org/average-cost-of-a-masters -degree.

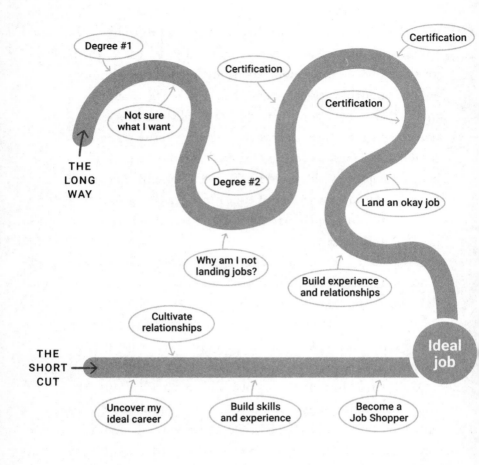

Now, Gail was a trouper. She trusted my coaching and discovered that she'd love a job in research. In a matter of weeks, we had repositioned her LinkedIn profile to where she was getting five contacts a week from recruiters asking Gail to interview for roles (that she had never applied for!) in her new target field. In the end, she landed a high-profile research role at a top university with a 33 percent salary increase. All of this done with Job Shopping strategies and no additional education.

Gail's situation is what I see from so many career changers and struggling job seekers. If a professional is struggling to land job offers, they may feel that they need additional education or training to make them stand out. This is usually because they are at a loss for what else to do. The answer is actually surprisingly simple: build experience and relationships. Now, you might be thinking, "But, Madeline, don't I need a job to gain more experience?" Fear not; in later chapters, I'll let you in on the secret sauce of putting yourself in front of the right people and creating experience without scoring a new role. Experience and relationships are the things that hiring managers actually value, not the extra diplomas gathering dust on your wall.

Myth 3: "The job search is a numbers game."

Before online applications, people would type out their résumés, print out a stack on paper so thick you could build a fort, and then shell out precious coins for the postage or transportation to get that résumé physically into the hands of hiring managers. This led to a lower volume of applications because people were more deliberate about where they chose to apply.

Fast-forward to the era of online applications, and companies are now completely inundated with them. The vast majority of the applications are the equivalent of spam in your email inbox: they are submitted by job seekers who likely haven't read the job description and are completely unqualified.

> *The online application process made it easier for job seekers to apply but harder to get noticed.*

When I asked recruiters at top tech companies how many of their hires come from online applications, they reported hiring only 10 to 15 percent of their workforce from that source. I spoke with a recruiter for a top streaming service who said that the number of applications would get so overwhelming to sort through that she would sometimes skip applications altogether and start searching on LinkedIn for the professionals with the right skill sets for the roles she was hiring for and simply invite those people to interview. This isn't unique to that company; many organizations with desirable or highly specialized roles employ dedicated sourcing teams to find the right candidates themselves instead of wading through the digital slush pile.

It certainly is possible to land a job by applying online. This is especially true if you directly meet the qualifications of the role (i.e., if you are coming from the same industry and held the same or similar role in the past).

> *But if only 10 percent of roles are filled by applying online, then applying online should be only 10 percent of your strategy.*

My client Nestor came to me with a master's degree and great transferable skills as a researcher, but had applied to five hundred jobs without landing a single offer. I really admired his dedication, yet my heart broke for him; I wished we had worked together sooner so I could have saved him all that time!

Nestor's situation is common, though. Many people apply to hundreds of jobs before landing an offer, and many people giving career advice online encourage this, telling followers to apply to dozens of jobs *every week*. But let me tell you a secret: the job search is not a numbers game. If it were, Nestor would have landed his job by applying online.

Imagine if the promise of this book was *"Try Job Shopping—it works less than 1 percent of the time!"* There's no way you would read it, right? And yet, that's the effectiveness of online applications—a statistical risk that would make even the boldest gambler hesitate.

Nestor decided to embrace the art of Job Shopping. He shifted from casting a wide net to carefully curating his job pursuits. The result? Interviews at one out of every three places he was interested in. Ultimately, he secured his dream role in a different career as an organizational development specialist with a $35,000 salary increase!

One of the key attributes of Job Shoppers is their focus on a low-volume job search. As a Job Shopper, you do not apply to hundreds of jobs like Nestor did at first. Instead, you focus on a small number that actually match what you are looking for (and land interviews at many of them!).

Myth 4: "I need to stay open to many different types of roles so I don't miss out on potential opportunities."

It may seem like being open to many different types of roles would increase your chances of getting hired. You might feel that you could miss out on a great opportunity if you limit your search to only one path. It's like thinking, "Why settle for one fish when you can cast a net big enough to catch the whole ocean?" But in the realm of job hunting, casting a wide net is, ironically, one of the top reasons you're not currently swimming in a sea of job offers.

Many job seekers who do this are multi-passionate professionals. These are folks who have a wide range of skills and interests and feel restricted by the idea that they have to specialize their skills and choose one path. Unfortunately, if you brand yourself to employers as a human Swiss Army knife, they will assume you are good at many things but great at nothing and will not hire you to solve their specific challenges. Companies are looking to hire an MVP—Most Valuable Player, not Most Vague Placeholder.

Some job seekers may be unsure about their career goals and may not know what they want to do next. As a result, they apply to a wide variety of jobs to see if any of them result in interviews. Back in my recruiting days, we once opened applications for an executive assistant position. I came across

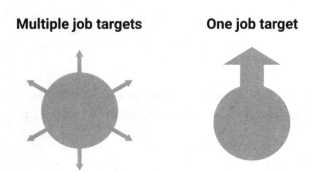

Multiple job targets   **One job target**

an accountant who was interested in the role, and I extended her an interview since I understood that her transferable skills could make her a good assistant. But in the interview, it became clear she hadn't thought much about this career change. I asked her, "Accountant to executive assistant, that's a big career change. What steps have you taken to be sure that being an executive assistant is the right role for you?"

She responded with "Well, this interview! I saw the job description, thought it sounded interesting, and so I took the call to learn more."

This is the last thing an employer wants to hear. This leads to a pretty quick rejection from the employer's side because they do not want to take a chance on hiring someone who isn't sure if they want the job. A company only wants to hire someone who has deeply considered their career possibilities and has fully and enthusiastically committed themselves to this path. Essentially, showing that you're open to many different roles sends up major red flags to employers that you will be difficult to retain. And honestly, it's not worth the challenge.

> *Employers do not want to be your career experiment.*

Needless to say, that was her first and final interview for that role.

To be clear, this isn't about having the right qualifications or not. Career changers who worked in completely different roles and industries can come across as completely confident in their next career move. It is near impossible to change careers if you aren't conveying this confidence to employers. They are already taking a chance on hiring someone who hasn't worked in this field before; if on top of it you're treating this as a career experiment, they are going to run in the other direction.

> *Soul search before you job search. It will save you so much time in the long run and lead to more satisfying results.*

Myth 5: "Things will eventually become clear, and it will all work out."

Among unsatisfied professionals, there's a recurring theme—the belief that someday (a mysterious day in the future) things will miraculously change and they'll stumble into the perfect job or career. At the same time, they (typically) do little to meaningfully alter their current situation. They don't like their job, so what do they do? Head to job boards and search for roles with a similar job title, hoping that the universe will sprinkle a bit of magic on their career if they just hit the refresh button in a different department or company. Efforts like this make professionals feel like they are doing something, when really they're just setting themselves up to take a new role and quickly become just as disenchanted as they were before. It's like rearranging deck chairs on the *Titanic*—it might seem like progress, but it's still the same old sinking ship. You've got to completely switch up your approach. If you keep playing the same game, you'll win the same prizes.

Melissa Ong, who gained fame in the early 2020s making short comedic videos on social media, has shared publicly how she came to determine that becoming an entertainer was the right career move for her. When she was a teenager, the influential voices in her life led her to believe her career options were limited to three things: technology, business, and medicine. Melissa chose technology since it was, in her words, "the option I hate the least."

This is the first misstep that leads so many people to feel passive in their careers: they don't know what opportunities are out there for them. Unfortunately, sometimes parents and society impose ideas of what they think you should be doing, but once you become a Job Shopper, you can see that your options are so much wider than you were once taught to believe.

After college, Melissa took a user experience (UX) design role at Yahoo and ended up deeply dissatisfied. She assumed she wasn't happy because she wasn't at the most coveted place to work (which if you asked anyone in tech at that time, they'd usually name one company: Google). Lo and behold, when she did snag a role at Google, she discovered a whole new level of job discontent. Google's high-performance culture hit her like a freight train, leading to a mental breakdown three months into the gig. It turns out, the grass isn't always greener, especially if it's covered in the high-performance fertilizer of Google.

The fatal mistake Melissa made here is she didn't look before she leaped. A common misstep that job seekers make is they fall in love with the idea of a company but haven't done the due diligence of understanding what the day-to-day would look like in that job.

You don't need to take a job to know whether or not it's a good fit for you.

Melissa's story has a happy ending. She found comedy and has been a successful performer and content creator. But just imagine if she had been a Job Shopper and taken control of her career sooner. She wouldn't have had the years of stress, despair, and confusion.

Your career is one of the most important decisions you'll make in your life. The role you are in impacts not only your salary but also your personal relationships, health, lifestyle, and happiness. This is not the time to take a backseat approach.

Job Shoppers do not sit around and think, "Well, I don't love working here but I just got a promotion. Maybe I'll stick it out for a bit and see if things will get better." Life is too short to do something that doesn't light you up. Even if you don't know what it is yet, you need to be relentless until you figure it out.

Leaving Behind These Myths Is Easier Said Than Done

So, congratulations, you've now mentally dumped these job search myths! But let's be realistic: a couple of them are probably clinging to your brain like stubborn glitter. To expect you to completely change your job search now, even armed with these revelations, is unrealistic, so don't beat yourself up if you still see these myths creeping in as you continue your job search. It's going to take a bit of time for you to move your mindset in this new direction. You've got old habits you need to shed, so in acknowledging this difficulty, we lay the groundwork for genuine transformation—the kind that propels us beyond the comfort zone and into the realm of Job Shopping.

We've busted five myths that are lingering around the job market like persistent rumors. Dispelling the misconception that aiming lower makes the process easier, challenging the belief that more degrees or certifications guarantee success, and debunking the numbers game mentality are crucial steps toward a more effective job search. Additionally, we've warned against the scattered, open-to-anything approach, because job hunting is not a buffet where you pile your plate with everything just because it's there. And finally, we learned to soul search before you job search. The right job rarely falls from the sky; you've got to do the hard work of figuring out exactly what that is. (But don't worry, I'll help you figure this out in chapter 3.)

In this book, I will assert over and over that you do not want to take a passive approach to your career. You may fear change. You may lack confidence in your abilities. You may not have clear career goals. You may doubt the right job is even out there for you. You may not know where to start. But it doesn't matter. I believe deeply that this isn't a part of your life that you can leave up to chance. And this is the importance of becoming a Job Shopper—you get to take control!

Key Takeaways

- Aiming for roles below your skill level in your job search isn't a shortcut to success. Companies are wary of overqualified candidates since they fear you will ask for a promotion or salary increase quickly, or simply leave when a higher-level job becomes available.

- Degrees and certifications rarely help you to stand out, and instead are more of a baseline qualification. While prestigious degrees can matter in certain fields, for most jobs, experience and relationships are what catch the company's attention.

- Focus on quality instead of quantity in job applications. It's not about blasting out as many applications as possible. Focus on fewer opportunities that truly match your skills and interests, and then put sincere effort into landing those interviews.

- Casting a wide net in your job search can backfire. Employers can tell when you aren't sure what you want next in your career, and they will reject you for it.

- Actively shape your career. Waiting for clarity to magically appear won't lead you to your dream job. Take proactive steps to explore different opportunities, conduct thorough research, and make informed decisions about your career path.

Chapter 2

THE JOB SHOPPER ADVANTAGE

When I worked in recruiting, we opened a marketing intern role. If you've ever posted an internship job opening, you know the flurry of incoming applications feels like you've tossed breadcrumbs to a pond of hungry ducks. I knew that I would be wading through an endless pool of people who simply saw the words "paid internship" and didn't give a second thought to applying. A friend of mine, Jessie, recommended I put a simple direction in the job description to see who actually read it.

So, in the job description, I asked applicants to put the price of Ethereum that day in the free response area of the application. The company was in the cryptocurrency industry, so I thought this would be a simple task relevant to something they should be keeping tabs on. The answer was able to be found with a quick Google search, and I wasn't looking for the "right" answer, I was simply looking at "Did you actually read this before applying?"

The results of how many people followed instructions was disappointing, to say the least.

A whopping 80 percent of applicants either did not read or did not fully read the job description, and upon closer inspection, I found they had no real resemblance to candidates meeting the qualifications. I shared this finding on social media, and recruiters were quick to chime in that they were not at all surprised:

- "These figures are similar to what I've experienced. I've even seen close to 90% of people being unqualified."
- "Coming from someone who screens hundreds of résumés, this is accurate. Most applications are either not in the right geography or don't qualify at all."
- "As a former hiring manager, for even say 100 applicants that cleared the ATS* to reach a short-list review by me—I might only move 5–10 forward for a screening interview."

And when we all say "unqualified" I want to be clear: they meet fewer than 50 percent of the requirements. And it's usually far less than that. Because I open my arms to career changers who are making an intentional shift with their transferable skills. But this ain't that.

---

* ATS (applicant tracking system) software is a tool recruiters use to help them organize talent, track interview processes, make offers, and hire.

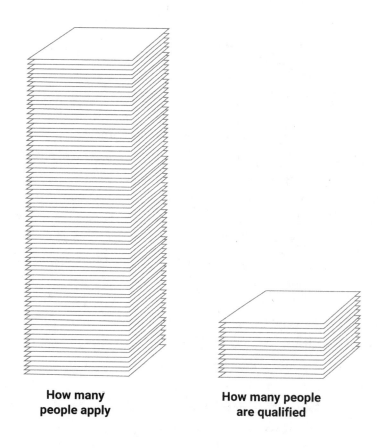

**How many
people apply**

**How many people
are qualified**

If you're listening closely, you'll hear this is actually a wonderful opportunity for you. Instead of getting discouraged when you see how many hundreds of people have already applied for an open role, rejoice in the fact that the pool of true competition for that job is actually much smaller. This is part of the reason why job candidates have more leverage than you think.

Job Shoppers Have Leverage, Even in an Employer's Market

Depending on the job market conditions, I often hear people question whether or not they are still able to be a Job Shopper. These questions tend to come up if unemployment is high, layoffs are frequent, the economy is taking a nap, technology seems to be replacing jobs, and so on. And these are fair questions: over and over in your career, the employment landscape will be deemed an "employer's market," meaning there are more job seekers than there are desirable jobs.

Sure, on a macro level you may experience an employer's market, but that's when Job Shopping becomes your greatest asset. It is what makes you more competitive and helps you stand out in tough times. Most Job Shoppers can see the positive benefits for themselves: they get to be choosy about their next opportunity and have companies sell to them.

But what might not be as immediately obvious is that Job Shopping actually benefits the company, too. Job Shopping perfectly aligns with a company's hiring goals, because they want to find a mutual fit just as much as you do! Companies love this approach of finding a mutual fit, and, armed with the strategies in this book, you'll become a completely irresistible candidate in an otherwise crowded market.

> *Because here is the thing: while job seekers optimize to reduce time, companies optimize to reduce risk.*

No job seeker wants their time wasted, and it's grueling to send out applications without any promise that the time spent will manifest into opportunities. You also don't want a hiring process that takes so much time and energy that it feels equivalent to serving jury duty for a drawn-out case.

But companies do this because they are optimizing to reduce risk. All those hoops they have you jump through is because they don't want to be too hasty and put a metaphorical ring on it unless they for sure know you're the one.

This is where Job Shopping blows everyone else out of the water. While other job seekers accidentally slip red flag phrases into their job interviews, Job Shoppers confidently present a future the company can see them in, one aligned with the company's expectations. This eases the crippling anxiety hiring managers have about making the wrong choice, because the Job Shopper takes all the hard thinking out of it.

It's like when I became a new parent and had to navigate the stroller market—a million options, all with different features, and a price tag that made my wallet break into nervous hives. If there could have been a stroller angel that sat on my shoulder at that moment and said, "Madeline, my understanding is that you value X, Y, and Z in a new stroller. I know exactly which one you should get and I'll walk through why it's the right fit for your needs." Well, consider me sold.

That's what Job Shoppers do. They aren't so focused on playing the numbers game or impressing the hiring manager with all the great things they've done. No. They understand the job at hand and confidently convey how they are the right fit to tackle it.

Therefore, when a Job Shopper paints this future where they are solving the company's challenges, the company will pay a premium to hire that Job Shopper over anyone else. Even when they have other, less expensive hiring options!

Leverage Isn't Reserved for a "Type" of Candidate

When I speak in a starry-eyed manner about this "Job Shopper" ideal, job seekers are quick to provide me with a long list of reasons why it isn't realistic or won't work for them, including:

- "I don't have a prestigious degree."
- "I'm a career changer."
- "I'm too early in my career."
- "I'm too late in my career."
- "I don't have brand names on my résumé."
- "That only works for certain professions."

But from helping thousands of my clients to go from job seeker to Job Shopper, I know it's possible for you, despite those additional barriers in your way.

Talk about barriers: one of my clients, Alanna, came to me when she was six months pregnant and looking for a new job. She knew she had to be honest with the companies she was interviewing with—anything beyond a phone interview and it was clear that she was going to have a baby. She was seen as a risky candidate on the surface—most companies don't want to hire someone new only for them to take time off immediately.

When Alanna joined my coaching program she was exhausted—she had been sending out twenty applications a day and was well past looking for the perfect job. She was feeling hopeless. Anything would do at this point.

Alanna works in corporate training and development, and

with Job Shopping coaching, her entire approach transformed. The biggest change was she had the language to talk about herself in a way that reflected her true value.

Alanna went from zero job offers to landing *nine* offers! They knew she was pregnant and continued to bid and compete for her to accept their offer. One company told Alanna that she was unanimously their number one choice and they would do anything to make her able to start with the company. This included a flexible schedule, with the ability to start as a consultant, take maternity leave, and then come back as a full-time employee—anything to get her to say yes.

So many people start where Alanna was—exhausted, working so hard in the job search, and facing more rejection than a puppy trying to befriend a cat. But the magic of Job Shopping is that *you* don't need to change. You are valuable. You have a great attitude, work ethic, and talent. It's just your approach that needs to change. It's a skill that you need to build. And you've spent your whole life building new skills; now it's time to build this one.

I could continue through a long list of success stories of people with unfavorable situations who got extraordinary results through Job Shopping, but at a certain point you have to realize: this success isn't reserved for the elite and privileged. Yes, your life has significant obstacles, and they *do* make landing a job more difficult. That rich boy who is a third-generation Stanford grad and whose mommy is a senior vice president at Merrill Lynch very likely has an easier time landing a cushy job than you. But what I'm saying is that you can have more, and you can do more. You can compete in another league than you're playing in now.

You Are Not a Commodity

It's wild. When I helped teams hire, we would get hundreds of applications, be in desperate need for someone to take over the vacant workload, and have a limited budget for compensation—and still end up searching high and low for candidates, interviewing for months, and finally extending an offer to the favorite candidate for $10,000 more than the top of our range.

Why? Because skilled professionals aren't commodities. They are not interchangeable. Each candidate has a unique combination of skills, character, and attitude. People often think it's just the skills that a hiring team evaluates, but it's all of those factors, and an experienced hiring manager knows that if they compromise on any of them, they are setting themselves up for a much more challenging situation later. In this day and age, companies with the most people or the fastest time to hire don't win. It's the companies with the best talent, sharpest minds, and most dedicated workers.

For example, I once conducted a tough search for a product designer. The role was challenging to fill because the person had to have the technical skills, but also a refined eye for design.

When we advertised the opening we were fortunate to receive three hundred applications. As I painstakingly went through each one, only nine met the specific qualifications the hiring manager had laid out. We narrowed it down to our top choice, but the catch was, she lived in another state. If we wanted her, we would have to pay thousands in relocation costs and wait four weeks for her to join the team. The budget was tighter than a pair of early 2010s skinny jeans and we urgently needed the help, yet we still went with her.

It sounds counterintuitive at first, but the short-term pain of paying $4,000 in moving costs and waiting four weeks is worth it in the long run to get a quality hire. Heck, $40,000 and two months, depending on the role and company, is an easy exception to make for a high performer.

When you're a Job Shopper, companies will make these easy decisions for you as well. Even if you have something that makes you a less ideal candidate, as long as you are able to paint a future for them where only you are in it, they will make exceptions.

And while the candidate we chose was a Job Shopper and got what she wanted, the company got exactly what it wanted, too. Upon writing, this candidate still works at the company six years later and has been promoted three times. If that's not a sign that we made the right decision, I don't know what is.

You Have More Power Than You Think

At one point in my career I was laid off unexpectedly. Yes, even the captain of the HR ship can be tossed overboard. Leading up to this, the CEO had been telling me—for many months—"Don't leave the company, we're likely to get acquired, and your HR leadership is an important part of the acquisition." Then one day, half of the company were gathered together, and we were all terminated on the spot.

If you've ever been laid off (especially in the United States), you know that the experience is utterly disorienting.

I felt like the floor fell out from under me, and it was so heartbreaking to leave a place where I had spent three years. I adored the work and my colleagues.

But I wasn't mad at the company, nor was I mad at the CEO. From my perspective as an HR executive, I'd seen the underbelly of a business and the gut-wrenching decisions businesses have to make in order to stay alive during tough times. And because I had this behind-the-scenes knowledge of what businesses do when facing a sudden changing tide, I had planned for this.

I had been practicing Job Shopping strategies for a year. The next week, I had four job interviews lined up, all with promising companies. Then, within three weeks of being laid off, I had three job offers.

Job security isn't guaranteed, so instead, you need to build Career Security.

Career Security, as I define it, is setting yourself up to make a career move at any moment, should your employment or financial situation decline. It is having a personal brand, marketable skills, and a strong network. We'll discuss how to build Career Security in more detail in chapter 10, but for now, it's good to keep in mind that this is ultimately what becoming a Job Shopper builds toward.

> *The best time to be a Job Shopper and build Career Security is before you need to move jobs, but the next best time is right now.*

There is incredible power in knowing that even if a boss is toxic, the company runs low on money, or something in your life suddenly requires you to move, you can seamlessly start a job search where companies are competing to have you join them.

Job Shoppers have Career Security because they prepare themselves to be marketable employees with clear next steps and strategies, before they find themselves playing musical chairs with jobs.

When I was laid off, my ability to land a job very quickly was a year in the making. Ideally, you become a Job Shopper before you feel your job is in danger. But if you're already on the job market, don't worry—you can still expedite your job search dramatically with the right steps, laid out in this book.

> *Since the company you work for owns your job, you need to own your career.*

Career Security is the outcome of being a strong Job Shopper both when you're looking for a job and when you're not.

So what do you do with this information? You need to market yourself in the job search as if you're in a league of your own. Your greatest asset is that there is only one of you. You are completely unique. If you can show an employer how you can uniquely fit into their team and provide the solutions they need, you'll be set. So let's get started.

Key Takeaways

- Even in an employer's market, focus on finding a mutual fit and aligning with hiring goals by demonstrating how you can provide unique value to employers.

- Proactively prepare for career transitions by adopting Job Shopping strategies to ensure readiness for potential changes in employment status.

- Build Career Security by enhancing marketability, developing a personal brand, acquiring in-demand skills, and expanding your network.

Chapter 3

UNCOVERING YOUR NEXT CAREER STEP

n 2024, I ran a poll of over three thousand people asking
them how they chose the career they are currently in.

Ten percent chose their career because of family and societal pressures—this was lower than I expected.

Another 14 percent of people chose their career because
they "explored until [they] found the right one." This was
the answer I was hoping for, and it's the Job Shopper way,
but it is unfortunately rare. This exploration is very difficult
to do without a plan and strategy. (Hint: by the time you
implement what is in this book, you will be in this category.)

Twenty-two percent chose their career because they "followed [their] passion." This is an approach that sounds good
at first, but leads to a lot of disappointment.

If you're doing the math along with us at home, that leaves
54 percent of people who chose the answer "I stumbled into
it." Arguably one of the most important decisions of your

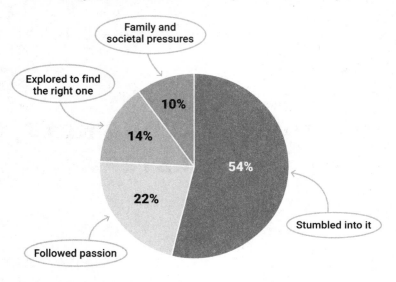

How did you choose the career you are currently in?

Family and societal pressures — 10%

Explored to find the right one — 14%

Stumbled into it — 54%

Followed passion — 22%

life, and the majority of people choose to "not choose" and instead stumble into something. Excuse me while I go scream into my pillow.

I will say, I knew before I ran this poll that stumbling into careers was common, but I didn't realize the situation was that dire. This approach to your career is easy in the short term (you don't have to put in the hard work of figuring out what to do), but much more difficult in the long run.

This approach of stumbling from one opportunity to the next is like hitchhiking through your career. You step out onto the road, stick your thumb out (a.k.a. apply to a bunch of opportunities), and whichever opportunity stops to pick you up, that's the direction your career is now driving in. Instead, I want you to plot your path and get in that driver seat. I want you to know where you're going and not let anyone else be in control. That's what this book is for.

The Lazy River

When people are successful in a career path they stumbled into, I call it being on the "lazy river." They are sitting in their inner tube, following the flow of the river of their career. They are good at their job, so they get offered a promotion. They don't really like their job that much, but think, "I would be crazy not to take the promotion, right?" And then they don't change their job for several years as they take on this new role. This goes on for another promotion, and then they get an email from a recruiter at another company. This new company is offering more money and a bigger title.

The person still doesn't like their job much, but again, they think, "Well, what else would I do in my career? And am I willing to start over? Maybe taking this new job will be different." They continue to ride that inner tube down the lazy river.

Twenty years go by and the light has gone out of their eyes. They are making good money, have a good title, and are good at their job. They wonder why they are still so unhappy when from the outside, everything looks perfect. They should be grateful, shouldn't they?

This is the false comfort that will eat away at your soul for years. This is your moment to hop out of that inner tube!

Now, it's easier said than done. When you start exploring what your next career move should be, you are going to hit a lot of dead ends. This is so frustrating, because when you

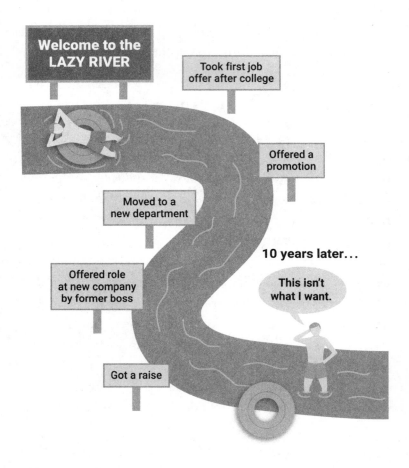

actually get real about what you want in your career, most of the jobs you thought you would be interested in end up not being the right fit. It's like going on a hundred first dates to finally find your soulmate—it's easy to feel on date 99 that the person isn't out there.

> *The reality is, in the job search process, figuring out what you want is often the most difficult part.*

People are astounded when they see the dramatic career shifts my clients of all ages have made. I've changed college professors into product managers, accountants into researchers, and relationship coaches into customer success managers. Any transformation is possible, but it all breaks down if you haven't done the prework of understanding who you are and what you want. This is the first real step of Job Shopping. (We will discuss figuring these things out in just a bit with what I like to call the Well-th Formula.)

Knowing exactly what job you want before you start your job search is crucial for several reasons. First, it saves time and energy. Many job seekers are too busy chopping down trees to sharpen their axes. They obsessively apply to a wide array of jobs, with the mentality that they can't slow down because they need a job quickly. Yet, getting focused dramatically decreases their job search time. Trust me on this one. Dozens of applications turn into single digits, and companies ask Job Shoppers to interview without having to apply.

Second, the way you convey your value and build your expertise is so impactful when you have direction. You're reading the right books, attending the right events, building the right side projects, all in service to be a 10/10 hire in your chosen field. And it shows.

Third, if your online presence and résumé all convey one specific expertise, you'll get more interviews and offers, full stop. A Job Shopper zeroes in on their next career move and then doesn't dilute their message with a broad value proposition.

Finally, knowing what you want will make you happier. I

am talking about steady, sustaining, look-forward-to-Monday happiness. Three jobs have made me feel this way in my career, and if you haven't felt this way, boy, you're in for a treat!

Stop Following Your Passions

Before we dive into the nitty-gritty of narrowing down what is your next career step (I swear, we are getting to it!), it's so important to shed the false notion of what a "dream job" looks like. We often get distracted with notions like "Find a job you love and you'll never work a day in your life." This idea, as well as the similarly trite suggestion "Follow your passion," is a harmful mischaracterization of what having a great job is.

Jobs are to make money, first and foremost. Let's not confuse them with our hobbies and leisure. Work will feel like work. So do dream jobs even exist?

Absolutely! I've had several dream jobs. My clients consistently land them. But a clear distinction is that Job Shoppers don't see dream jobs as doing our hobbies all day.

I don't have clients who are looking to get paid to announce tennis matches, play video games, or cuddle pandas.

No, instead we see a dream job as:

- A job that energizes us
- A paycheck and lifestyle that allow us to enjoy what we love outside of our job
- Work that feels meaningful
- A company with people who we respect and trust

WHAT WE THINK IS A DREAM JOB	WHAT IS ACTUALLY A DREAM JOB
Doing work related to our hobbies and interests	Doing work that addresses our strengths and values
Experiencing a role that fits our life's purpose	Experiencing meaningful work, but, more importantly, allowing us the time and money to provide meaning in other aspects of our lives
Working at a popular company	Working at a company with great people
Feeling like we are never working	Having work that gets us frequently into a flow state
Having high status and access to flashy events, people, or perks	Having high satisfaction in our overall life and limited stress

This version of a dream job is 100 percent possible for you.

You're not sentenced to stay at a job just because you're good at it and nothing's glaringly wrong. You, my friend, deserve better.

While knowing what job you want is a key component to being a Job Shopper who stands out from the competition, above all, this is about life satisfaction. I want you to land the greatest job of your life and have a fulfilling career from here on out. Sure, you may have taken jobs in the past that ended up not being a good fit for your lifestyle, had a poor work culture, or didn't fit your strengths—but that's never going to happen again. You hear me?

In this chapter, we are going to walk through how to figure out exactly what you want in your career in record time, using the Well-th Formula.

The Well-th Formula

The Well-th Formula will help you to uncover your ideal career path by showing you who you are and what jobs will match your needs. The three components to the formula are values, strengths, and market demand. With these three things in alignment, you'll make the best possible career move.

> *Values + Strengths + Market Demand = Well-th*

Why do I misspell "wealth" like that? Because a Well-thy life is about not just living rich but living well. Yes, first and foremost I want you to make good money that allows you to live a comfortable lifestyle. But a Well-thy life is also one where you have the time and energy to do the things you want to do. For some people it means having time flexibility. For others it means closing their computer at five p.m. and not looking at it until the next day. For others it means every month you're in a different city. Whatever that is, that is the life you are going to build as a Job Shopper.

So let's walk through the three pillars of the Well-th Formula.

Values

Vishal, an avid gamer and technology enthusiast, dreamed of landing a job as a software engineer in the video game industry. He spent months applying to gaming companies and attending gaming conventions, hoping to turn his passion into a career.

He initially became my client to get to the finish line with a gaming company, but ended up getting a very different result. I had him go through a process called the "One Page Career Vision," which helped him find clarity around what his next career move should be and the path to get there. One of the exercises he did is the one I'm about to share with you: with it, he got clear on his values.

Vishal talked to people in the gaming industry who were doing the jobs he wanted, and as they described their work, he realized it contradicted his values. All of the people he spoke to reported long working hours, excessive crunch periods, and a lack of work-life balance. This culture can contribute to high stress levels, burnout, and mental health issues. Of course, this doesn't mean if you work in the video game industry you are doomed to this fate, but the pattern was pretty apparent based on the conversations Vishal had with those professionals.

Vishal began to think that he was possibly confusing his love of games with a love of *working* in games.

He took a deeper look at what mattered to him for his next opportunity, realized that he could have everything he wanted in a different type of industry, and prioritized having a job that allowed him the free time to play video games and have gaming side projects.

Vishal ultimately found that what truly brought him joy was using technology to solve real-world problems. He shifted his focus and eventually accepted a position as a software developer in a company that specialized in creating educational apps for children. Though not as glamorous as working for a gaming giant, Vishal found immense fulfillment in knowing that his work was making a positive impact on young minds and fostering their love for learning.

Additionally, since it was a company focused on children, many of the employees were parents, so work–life balance and reasonable hours were ingrained in the culture. Vishal found a job that was true to his values and that allowed him the free time to game and the income to upgrade all his gear.

Like Vishal, your job search could be speeding toward opportunities that violate your values and you don't even know it! Move through the following steps to uncover your career values:

Step 1. Write out the top things you value in a job. Here are some examples of values. Feel free to adopt some of them for your list, and to come up with your own:

Advancement	Autonomy	Balance	Commute
Creativity	Diversity and Inclusion	Family Time	Flexibility
Innovation	Interpersonal Relationships	Organizational Ethics	Prestige
Professional Growth	Risk	Stability	Variety

Ask yourself these questions to guide you as you create your list:

- What gives my work a sense of meaning or enjoyment?
- What kind of lifestyle do I envision for myself, and how does work fit into that vision? What kind of money, time, and energy would I need to make that possible?
- What types of work environments do I thrive in?
- Where do I see my career five years into the future? What would need to happen in my next job in order to arrive at that future?
- How does this job align with my overall well-being, both physically and mentally?
- What are features of jobs and work cultures that I've disliked in the past and do not want to relive?

Here's an example of how your answers to these questions can help you decipher what values are most important to you:

- What gives my work a sense of meaning or enjoyment?
  - ▶ *The feeling of learning something new.*
    Value: Professional Growth

- What kind of lifestyle do I envision for myself, and how does work fit into that vision? What kind of money, time, and energy would I need to make that possible?
  - ▶ *Buying a home and being able to afford a housekeeper.*
    Value: High Earning Potential

- What types of work environments do I thrive in?
  - ▶ *Social environments where I build relationships with my coworkers.*
    Value: Interpersonal Relationships

- Where do I see my career five years into the future? What would need to happen in my next job in order to arrive at that future?
  - ▶ *I'd like to be director-level. I'd need opportunities to take on stretch projects.*
  - *Value:* Professional Growth

- How does this job align with my overall well-being, both physically and mentally?
  - ▶ *I need it to be at a place that values diverse voices and backgrounds.*
  - *Value:* Diversity and Inclusion

- What are features of jobs and work cultures that I've disliked in the past and do not want to relive?
  - ▶ *I worked at a company where the CEO kept changing the product direction.*
  - *Value:* Strong Vision from Leadership

These questions will likely yield more than one value each. Heck, by the time you're done going through the questions you may have dozens of values. That's normal.

But, as with any brainstorming process, I am going to have to ask you to kill your darlings, my friend.

Because **Step 2** is to narrow them down to your top five values. While I understand that likely all fifteen of the values you listed are meaningful to you, you won't find them all in one job. That's why you must narrow down your values until you are left with your top five. Cross them off one by one. Then, once you have your final five, you are going to relentlessly look for a role that fits all five. Everything below this list of five, we can compromise on, but if a role or career path doesn't hit these top values, you'll need to walk away. This clarity will help you to make much more lucid career decisions.

So take some time to define your top five values. These will serve as guiding principles that will help you to choose the right industry, company, and role. When your work aligns with your values, it can lead to greater job satisfaction and a better overall sense of well-being.

Strengths

The next piece of the Well-th Formula is your strengths. Growing up, you might have tried basketball, swimming, and volleyball before deciding that swimming was going to be your sport. Why did you choose swimming? I'd be willing to bet it was the sport where you had the most natural talent. Because it came easily to you, you found it more enjoyable, and you were also able to excel at it more quickly than others.

People often try to find an enjoyable career by looking at their interests, like an audiophile wanting to coordinate a massive music festival, a fitness buff eager to launch a big sports apparel campaign, or a reality TV fan interested in writing the contracts for the contestants on a hit television show.

But those things don't tend to be as fun as they look. They are work, and too often this is the quickest way for you to start hating your hobbies. Instead, if you're looking for fun, look to build mastery. Because you know what's really fun? Being great at something and making a lot of money for it.

Think back to the things you've built mastery in, and how it got especially fun as you leveled up: When you learned all the rules to a board game and were able to develop a strategy that allowed you to win. When you went to that workout class six weeks in a row and seamlessly moved between exercises without the same level of effort as the newbies. When your absurd amount of knowledge of Greek mythology came in clutch during that one round of bar trivia where you proudly contributed many correct answers for your team.

This is what mastery feels like. When you have a natural inclination for something, it gets more fun the better you get. But it's not just about having a good time; when you play to your strengths, you'll get promoted faster, make more money, and more often get into a flow state where you lose track of time because you are so focused.

Contrast this to a job that does not play to your strengths. Take for instance when I worked in market research. Let's start off by saying: I am not detail-oriented. This job had me scouring pages and pages of data for inaccuracies, and then clicking through hundreds of surveys to find errors in the logic. When five p.m. rolled around each day I was absolutely exhausted. On the surface, it doesn't make much sense that sitting at a desk doing basic tasks all day would be exhausting, but it was because these duties went directly against my nature.

A weakness of mine is trying to focus on small details, so

it took a lot of effort to do these simple tasks. I would count down the moments until the end of the day and then leave work right at five because I couldn't stand to do the work any longer. The performance reviews I received were 2s and 3s out of 5s.

The next job I obtained was working in human resources. While there were some detail-oriented tasks I had to complete, they were balanced by things like revamping the onboarding process for employees. This work involved problem-solving, creativity, and understanding human behavior—three major strengths of mine. Time at that job flew by, and I was constantly coming up with new ideas for how to improve the department, and additional projects I could work on.

I was the same person, but with seemingly two completely different work ethics in those jobs.

It's all about the garden you are planted in. If you are a flower wilting in one garden, is it the fault of the flower, or are you perhaps not in the right garden, with the right soil, amount of sunlight, and temperature? You might just need to be replanted. The right garden will play to your strengths each day.

This is why the story of my time in market research might seem like quite the outlier to my workaholic, achievement-oriented personality. But the truth is, I have been truly successful only when I have played to my strengths. My secret is I know my strengths, and I lean heavily into improving them and spend much less time focusing on my weaknesses.

The funny thing is, while you may understand the importance of knowing your strengths intellectually, your next thought might be "Oh, snicklefritz, I don't know what my strengths are."

And that's okay! Many people don't know what their strengths are right off the top of their head, especially the strengths that companies will pay good money for. There are several ways to uncover your strengths. Here are a few:

1. TAKE A STRENGTHS ASSESSMENT.

There are several strengths assessments online that will give you a report of what your strengths are based on a series of questions you answer (I have updated links to a strengths assessment in the supplemental resources online at reversethe search.com/resources). Professionals tend to really enjoy these assessments because seeing their strengths described in a report helps them to see their abilities in a new light.

After getting your results, make sure to take the extra step to understand how your strengths translate to employable skills that companies are looking for. Let's say your strengths assessment says one of your strengths is "Philomath"—great, you love learning—but how does this translate to a line on a job description? Well, this has manifested itself in the fact that you are very quick to pick up new coding languages and are always staying up-to-date on the latest technology developments. Now that's an employable skill. Go through each of your strengths results and come up with one to three skills that have developed because of that strength.

2. ASK THE PEOPLE IN YOUR LIFE.

It can help to get an outside perspective when determining your strengths. You might be too close to the situation to see your own strengths clearly. Ask current and former coworkers and managers, "What are my strengths?" You will be surprised at how quickly those who have worked closely with you will rattle them off. Write down the names of five people who know your work style and reach out to them. You can say something like, "I could really use your feedback (and honestly a bit of an ego boost). What do you see as my top strengths?"

3. DO PERSONAL REFLECTION.

Take out a notebook and write down times when you felt most confident and successful in your work. Then identify what skills or abilities were responsible for that feeling. Write down positive feedback you have received from managers or colleagues, and look for patterns in what they have said.

Then answer these questions:

- What information do I naturally consume?
- What skills do I pick up easily?
- What am I good at that most people dread?

This final question gets to the overlap in the Venn diagram between what work you will enjoy and what you'll get paid good money to do. This is the sweet spot. This is what makes for a fulfilling career where you continue to get employment opportunities.

For example, one of my employees, Courtney, has the job of speaking with prospective clients to see if they would be a good fit for our coaching program. She is fabulous at it and makes a great living doing it. In a team meeting one day she disclosed that she was out to lunch with a friend, and when Courtney explained what her job entailed, her friend said, "That job sounds like an absolute nightmare. You talk to people all day?" It was such a great reminder that one person's dream job is another person's hellhole. Courtney's job is challenging, since working with clients isn't always smooth sailing, but she loves it. She is great at what other people dread.

Too often, people don't go deep enough when interpreting their strengths. They may observe: "One of my strengths is being a great performer. Okay, I'll be an actor, singer, or broadcast journalist." Unfortunately, that is firmly in the "many people enjoy this and there is a low demand for these skills" zone, so I challenge them to go deeper. What are the strengths that are under the surface of being a great performer? Those can often include communication, creativity, collaboration, and adaptability. By looking at these deeper strengths, new possibilities for career paths arise. A person like this could make a great sales representative, event planner, or advertising creative, just to name a few.

With all this in mind, it's now time to narrow down to your top five strengths.

Just like with values, five is the magic number to help you realistically find a role that plays to all of them. There will be strengths that you don't utilize in your career, and that's okay. Embrace them in your hobbies, social life, side hustle, and volunteer work. You will be happiest when you don't expect your job to meet every need.

One of the reasons I started posting content about the job search was because my job wasn't completely fulfilling me when it came to helping others and having a lot of creative freedom. Instead of going on the impossible quest of finding the perfect human resources job, I started my side hustle of career coaching. My employers will attest: my having a side hustle made me a better employee. I was highly satisfied at work. The highs and lows at work were more neutral for me because I wouldn't put my identity into projects, which could be crushing if they got canceled. I was already leading my own projects in my personal life, so I didn't need a work project to feel whole. I want you to find roles that play to your strengths, without the unrealistic expectation that your job needs to be your everything.

Market Demand

I wrote this book to get you paid, full stop.

A job is work. That certainly doesn't mean it can't be fun, enjoyable, and fulfilling, but at the end of the day, you're putting in effort for the paycheck.

Which brings us to market demand, the third element of the Well-th Formula.

Market demand means looking at the job market and understanding, for the jobs you're interested in:

1. How much does this career path pay at each stage in the career?
2. Are role openings increasing or decreasing?

Let's explore these questions.

HOW MUCH DOES THIS CAREER PATH PAY AT EACH STAGE IN THE CAREER?

Too often we choose a job that plays to our strengths, but it doesn't pay us the amount that we want to live a certain lifestyle. Do not go into a career that won't pay you enough. Period. I guarantee that you can find a career that you enjoy just as much as (or dare I say, more than) this job that underpays you.

For each career path you are considering, get an idea of what you'll be paid early, mid, and late in that career (or start at whatever point you're currently at in your career—no need to hear about entry level salaries if you'd go for director level roles). Many professions pay very little for entry level positions, but then have a steady incline in income as you jump to new levels. This is a good sign, because while you may be tempted to take a job that pays a lot out of the gate to entry level people, it's more important to look long term at your earning potential and compatibility with the job. Therefore I generally advise people looking at entry level roles to not choose one based on compensation, but rather on how much that role can set you on the right trajectory (and make that sweet money as you take higher jobs).

For other careers, you see that they pay low salaries for entry level jobs, then those barely tick up for midcareer, and maybe there are mild increases after ten years of being in the profession. I don't know about you, but that would be too slow for me to finally hit a level of income that I felt comfortable making. Of course, if your financial situation allows you to make less, then that can work for you, but few people have that luxury.

Early in my career I was on the path to becoming a journalist. The underlying message of every romantic comedy I watched growing up was that intelligent women become journalists. I had been subliminally primed to pursue this job since childhood.

So I tried my hand at it. But after working in journalism for only a bit, the rom-com illusions quickly faded. I began to wonder, Do I really want to live from deadline to deadline for little money and few employment opportunities? I did research on the market demand for journalists, and it was not good. Fewer openings each year; low pay throughout the career. I could have ignored that information and accepted that that would be my path in life because it was my "passion" and skill set. But I didn't want to accept that. Instead, I started exploring other jobs that I had no idea about but that I knew would pay me a lot better.

Similarly, my client Alice became a high school math teacher because she'd always had a natural talent for math and she values helping others. Despite loving her students, the dream came crashing down when she realized the market demand for teaching didn't match the lifestyle she wanted to lead: she wasn't making much money, and the path to making more money would be slow and far too gradual for her. Through following my strategies and coaching, we were able to help Alice to pivot successfully into data science. It was the perfect career path for her because it combined her analytical mindset, intellectual curiosity, and presentation abilities beautifully. Also, have you seen what data scientists get paid? Hint: it's more than a high school math teacher.

She landed an incredible data science job at an e-commerce company. One could say Alice sold her soul to do something less meaningful with her career. I'd disagree with that notion. Her new income and more flexible hours allow her to give back, including through involvement in organizations that get young women into technology. She gets so much fulfillment from mentoring high school students on data science to help them build the skills and confidence necessary to make a great living in the technology industry. Alice is thriving financially, she loves the company she works for, and she has the time and energy to give back in meaningful ways. I want this for you.

To understand the salary for a particular career, you can research the average salary for that role in different companies and locations using salary comparison websites (I have updated websites to do salary research at reversethesearch .com/resources), and you can also talk to people who work in the field and ask them about their pay and benefits. You can ask them something along the lines of:

- "Given your experience in this field, how much should someone in this path expect to make at each level?"

Focus on finding roles that have the right amount of pay to live a comfortable lifestyle at each stage of your career, while still honoring your strengths and values.

ARE ROLE OPENINGS INCREASING OR DECREASING?

Sure, the pay for the job you're interested in may meet your standards, but something that will make being a Job Shopper more effortless is building a career along a path that is increasing in demand year over year. I don't want you to gear up for a career move that in a few years is going the way of the dodo bird.

The world moves very quickly today, so it's important that you stay abreast of which skills are in demand, which are being replaced by technology, and which technologies you need to become adept at using. You likely won't stay in the same type of job for your entire career, but it's more natural to make modest pivots versus complete career overhauls. Because trust me, while career overhauls can be necessary (and many of my clients do them), it's much better to set out on a clear career path sooner, and re-skill later in minor ways.

To understand if a career field is growing, you can research the number of job openings and projections for future job growth in that field. You can check out websites like the Bureau of Labor Statistics (bls.gov), where you'll find the Occupational Outlook Handbook with information on specific careers and industries. When you search on job boards for roles, the sheer number of openings for different titles can give you clues. You can also talk to people who are in the profession and ask them how hard it is to land roles, and whether they see the roles being in demand for the future.

It's important before you dive into your next role that you have a clear understanding of what salary you'll be making and if jobs are being created in that field, rather than removed.

This isn't just for this next job move, but to set yourself up for success years into the future.

Putting the Well-th Formula into Action

It's time to get ultra clear on what direction your career is going and how you'll get there. While the Well-th Formula appears simple, to put it into action takes some time. Hopefully you have been following along and already started to compile these lists, but to recap your next steps:

1. Establish your top five values.
2. Establish your top five strengths.
3. Create a list of possible roles you could do.
4. Research each career path for market demand (eliminate those that immediately fail).
5. Speak with people in each of those roles (continue to eliminate options based on your strengths, values, and market demand).
6. Continue speaking with professionals until you've narrowed your next career move down to the one you want.

These steps may take you days to complete if you're already pretty sure about the next job you want, but they could take weeks if you aren't sure what you want yet upon reading this.

> *You want to be methodical about this process, because clarity creates speed.*

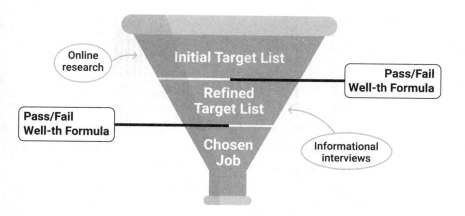

Only with clarity can you finally narrow the list of roles down to the single job that is the best fit for you—and the career you are going to pursue as a Job Shopper. I'll walk you through a few more things you'll need to know to complete this clarity process.

Choosing Target Roles

When you create a list of possible roles you could do, write down the first few obvious ones, but then go deeper. Many of the best jobs are not the obvious ones that we always think of. It reminds me of a woman I once met who was gushing about how much she loves her job. She works from home, gets paid great money, and has earned multiple promotions. What is the role? She is in quality assurance for a health insurance company. She got the job because she was a nurse and she works with providers to ensure they give quality care. My guess is that most people aren't familiar with what this job is.

Here are some ways to uncover nonobvious career paths (that are often even better than the obvious ones!):

1. Use online resources such as professional networking platforms, industry forums, and job search websites to explore a wide range of job titles. For example, I started scrolling through my local government's open job listings and saw many jobs I was unfamiliar with that paid great money. You can also go to a company's open roles and read through all of them instead of sorting by a filter.

2. Stay updated on industry reports and trend analyses. Emerging industries often come with innovative job titles. Keep an eye on sectors experiencing growth and transformation.

3. Conduct informational interviews with professionals in different industries. Ask about their roles, their responsibilities, and the skills required. This can help you discover unique job titles that may not be widely known.

4. Attend networking events, conferences, and meetups in various fields. Engage in conversations with professionals to learn about their job titles and the work they do.

5. Explore profiles on LinkedIn, paying attention to job titles and descriptions. You may come across titles that are not commonly heard of.

I want you to make a long list of potential next paths for yourself because a longer list forces you to find these jobs that you may not be aware of. You'll want to find jobs that are compatible with your strengths and values. You can start by doing some preliminary research about these roles to get a sense of what you would do in these jobs and understand the market demand.

However, where people go wrong is that they often stop at online research and then choose a job based on that. They assume that the only way they can understand if they'll like a job is if they work in it. That is not so. You must speak to people in those jobs to understand what it would be like.

Speaking with People in Potential Career Paths

You must speak to people in each of the jobs on your list that have survived the preliminary research round. It's likely that you don't have a personal contact in each job you're interested in, so you must ask your network to make introductions for you or do the ol' cold outreach to people with that background. For many of these roles, you'll speak with one person and see immediately that it is not the right path for you. This will be frustrating at times, but know that you're moving into Job Shopper territory when you realize you would hate to do most jobs. Most jobs don't even come close to meeting the requirements set out in the Well-th Formula.

As you talk to folks, you'll ask them questions about what they do all day, what the worst parts of their job are, and how much you should expect to earn at each stage in that career path (for an informational interview question guide, head to reversethesearch.com/resources). You'll craft your own questions based on whether the role will meet your strengths, values, and market demand, but above all, make sure you really get into the nitty-gritty of what this job entails. Picture yourself fully in the role, and be honest with yourself: Would this work make you miserable? Would it be okay? Or would it lead to a Well-thy career?

These informational interviews will be pivotal to uncovering your next move. Some of my clients speak to ten people and get clear on their next role; others speak to over fifty people. Don't stop until you have clarity.

This exercise is the secret to turbocharging your job search process. First, people love talking about themselves and feeling like they are helping others, so if you approach them as if they are a Sherpa guiding you through the unpaved path of your career, they'll enjoy imparting their knowledge (no matter your age!). Second, these people will become invested in your career journey, so they often become people who can help to refer you into jobs, if not now, then in the future.

Making Your Choice

After you've followed all the steps, it is time to make a decision. The worst thing you can do is *not* decide, leaving yourself in career purgatory with a passive career trajectory.

I put all these approaches into practice in my own career. When I was pivoting out of journalism, I considered how much I loved psychology. In school I would usually have to study hard to do well on tests, but somehow with psychology, all the concepts were so intuitive that I would easily ace exams. I had never felt that level of effortlessness for any other subject in my life. I considered what jobs people have who are good at psychology, and if you ask the typical person, they will suggest you become a therapist or researcher. Neither of those fit my values. I knew I wanted something more business-oriented where I could collaborate with a team and have high earning potential. So I set out to find other options.

The list of career paths I created was based on people who had the word "psychology" on their LinkedIn profile. If they were passionate about psychology, I wanted to know what career they'd settled on. I came across UX designers, school psychologists, human capital consultants, market researchers, and speech-language pathologists, to mention a few. I spoke with workers in all these professions and more by tapping alumni networks, reaching out to people online, and asking my friends, "What does your cousin/aunt/father do for a living?" to see if it was anything interesting to me.

One woman I contacted was a senior in my sorority when I was a freshman. We didn't really know each other, but she had a master's in human behavior and was working in human resources, a field I knew little about, so I asked if we could have a conversation. She was so gracious to say yes, and we met up for dinner the following week. As I asked her detailed questions about what she did for a living, it became increasingly apparent that I would love doing her job. I asked her for advice on how to get the right skills and make myself marketable in the field. Over the course of the next year I kept her in the loop of how I was utilizing her advice, as well as getting further insights from her.

When I was ready to hit the job market for a human resources role many months later, she referred me into a position at the company she worked for. That wasn't my grand plan all along, but it's amazing how often things can work out perfectly when you're making these connections!

This put my career on the right trajectory, and I followed this same process for every job in human resources after that. I continued to do informational interviews each time I was looking to change jobs, both to meet new people and to gain insight as to the type of company I should join next. This approach led me from dream job to dream job in HR.

Job Shoppers stay curious at each career move. They revisit their Well-th Formula and never stop doing informational interviews. This is what will unlock career happiness and a Well-thy life. The candidates that can articulate what they want out of a role, clearly understand their strengths, and know that the job is in demand come across as much more confident and self-assured in the interview process. Time after time, these candidates are the ones who get hired. They naturally make companies step up their game and focus on selling *them* on the role. Set your standards and allow companies to rise to them. And they will.

Key Takeaways

- Follow the Well-th Formula (Values + Strengths + Market Demand = Well-th) to explore career options, and avoid the common pitfall of basing career decisions on passion and interests.

- Values are your core priorities for your work and lifestyle. Create a list of values and then narrow it down to your top five.

- Strengths are what actually make work fun, because you build mastery with relative ease. Identify your top five strengths that you'd like to target for your next role.

- Market demand is understanding how much a role pays and if openings are increasing or decreasing. Research the salary trajectory and projections for future job growth for potential career paths to ensure compatibility with your lifestyle and financial goals.

- Create a comprehensive list of potential career paths, going beyond the obvious choices, and explore non-traditional job titles.

- Conduct informational interviews with professionals in various industries to gain insights into job responsibilities, possible challenges, and earning potential at each career stage.

- Continuously refine your career options based on your strengths, values, and market demand until you narrow down your choices to the most suitable role.

- Make an informed decision based on your research and insights gained from informational interviews, aiming for a career path that aligns with your values, utilizes your strengths, and offers growth opportunities.

Chapter 4

YOUR RÉSUMÉ ISN'T ABOUT YOU

once received a video résumé from a job candidate, and I'll
admit that I'm a total sucker for a candidate who goes above
and beyond. I eagerly clicked the video link, and this man
did end up on my list of most memorable candidates . . . but
not for good reasons.

The video begins with the candidate (let's call him Chris)
recounting his college years, where he studied music compo-
sition and theory. He shares his deep-rooted passion for music
and how it influenced his decision to pursue a career as a com-
poser. Chris highlights his early successes, such as scoring short
films and documentaries. He narrates the challenges he faced,
including the competitive nature of the industry and the need
to constantly evolve his skills—to the point where he began to
explore other career paths.

Okay . . . at this point we are two minutes into this video.
I want to watch Chris's whole video, but holy guacamole, he

applied for a *marketing* role. A couple minutes in and there's no sign that he even wants to be a marketer. While most recruiters would trash the résumé at this point, the job search coach in me has to see how it ends.

Chris spends the next two minutes outlining his proficiency in time management, creative problem-solving, and effective communication (awfully vague, isn't it?). He concludes by saying that he wants his next role to utilize these skills.

The video ends, and I bury my face in my hands.

> **Chris committed the cardinal sin that so many job seekers do: he made his application about himself, not what he can do for the company.**

Many job seekers don't understand the nuance that separates these two ideas, but this distinction is often the difference between landing the interview or not.

Frankly, companies aren't all that interested in your previous careers. What they do want to know is if you have the ability to rock the job they're hiring for. They also don't want to hear a vague list of talents and soft skills. Instead, they want to know that even if you're a career changer, you have prepared yourself to do *this* role, and that you can articulate exactly how you have the skills and can meet those goals.

> **We too often think of our résumé as a Wikipedia page. Instead, make it a sales page.**

Crafting a résumé that is compelling like a sales page is the first piece of branding that will transform you into a Job

Shopper and get companies coming to you with opportunities.

Let's explore how.

Autobiography Syndrome

I hate to inform you, but you may suffer from a very common condition called Autobiography Syndrome. Symptoms include telling your full career story to companies, including too many past roles on your résumé, and struggling to limit your résumé to one page.

Simply put, you're sharing too much. You view your résumé and other job seeker documents as an autobiography of sorts—chronicling each step of your career. And you do this for a good reason: you see your career as a complex mosaic of experiences that has made you the multifaceted professional you are today. A company can't fully understand how much of a gem you are without them seeing how your master's in architecture blossomed your creative and problem-solving skills, and then that door-to-door salesperson job crafted your ability to speak with anyone and persevere when things don't go as planned—it all adds up to you being a director of knowledge management, right? Kind of.

While those experiences have value, they are distracting when it comes to selling yourself to a hiring team. Your résumé becomes a long Wikipedia page of everything you've done because you are going for accuracy—you want to give them an accurate picture of everything they'll get when they hire you.

I had a client, Neil, who was going for product manager

roles, but see how he positioned himself on his LinkedIn profile:

> *Strategic Legal Professional and Persuasive Sales Maven Driving Tech Innovation as a Visionary Product Manager*

He then went into depth on his profile about how the merging of his legal and sales background made him an especially astute product manager. At that point, I had to diagnose him with a serious case of Autobiography Syndrome!

Let's break down what went wrong here.

1. He has distracted employers with terms like "legal professional" and "sales maven," which make interested parties much less likely to see him in the role he actually wants, product manager.
2. He thinks it's important to share the major parts of his background that happened before the career transition, when really, all they need to know is he's a product manager now and can do that job effectively.

The bottom line: he needed to stop positioning himself as what he used to be and start focusing on the value he was now offering the world. Neil struggled to do this—and I understand why. There is an element of mourning your past career work, those underutilized degrees, the skills you spent so much time mastering, and the reputation you built—that now all needs to be sidelined, since they are not the focus of the roles you are pursuing.

You may be a multi-passionate person like Neil, someone

who has a variety of skill sets and interests, and it's difficult to fit you in a box of one career path. That is beautiful, and it will serve you well in your career, but that long autobiography does not belong on your job search documents. Together, we'll craft a targeted résumé that will cure you of Autobiography Syndrome.

Speak to What the Company Is Looking For

The antidote to Autobiography Syndrome and the key to transforming your Wikipedia page into a sales page is starting with what a company is asking for in the job description and determining what information to share based on that. This is the antithesis of how most of us were taught to write a résumé.

Essentially the guidance we are given is: write down all the cool stuff you've done and use flashy adjectives to describe yourself, like "collaborative," "motivated," and "seasoned."

Please don't do this!

Many of my clients join my program after they have already hired a résumé writer and are completely disappointed by the results. Before joining the program, my client Liz hired a résumé writer to refresh her materials. She used her new résumé to apply to fifteen jobs and didn't land interviews at any of them, despite being perfectly qualified. The writer told her to apply to fifteen more and come back if she still didn't hear anything.

This advice really snags my zipper, because I would never tell a client to apply to that quantity of roles. We began working together and revamped her résumé (the right way). The major transformation came from speaking directly to what the companies she was interested in were looking for. She then translated these insights to her LinkedIn profile, and after we started working together, do you know how many places she applied to? Zero.

Liz instead became a magnet for opportunities. Her LinkedIn was popping off. She landed seven interviews—and then later three job offers—from companies that reached out to *her*, no application required. With the ability to weigh her options, Liz ultimately accepted a role with a more impressive title and 25 percent salary increase. You can do this, too, when your job search documents speak clearly to what companies are looking for.

Allow me to pull back the curtain as to what's happening when your résumé is reviewed by the hiring team, so you'll understand how to convey your value the right way.

When reviewing résumés, recruiters and hiring managers glance over the document quickly. They start at the top, looking at your name and skimming over your summary. They then shoot down the left side of the page, taking note of your job titles and company names, and then pause quickly to notice your education at the bottom. After this brief glance of no more than a few seconds, if you grab their attention, they will begin to read the contents of your résumé. They'll usually look at your summary section and then the first and possibly second bullet of your past few jobs.

> *If you put all of your experience on the résumé and simply hope that the recruiter will sift through it to find*

> *the relevant information they need, you will likely not land the job offer.*

This means that we need to catch their attention very quickly with the right positioning of your skills, which we will discuss in depth in the next few sections.

Find the GLORY in Your Story

Job seekers struggle to keep their résumés focused only on what the company wants to hear, which is why I created a foolproof method for writing the best possible résumé. It's called the GLORY Formula, and it includes the five steps you need to take to create your résumé.

> **GLORY** *Formula*
> **G***ather Keywords*
> **L***ist Tasks Performed*
> **O***bserve Your Story*
> **R***efine the Accomplishment*
> **Y***es Statements*

Through this process you will create your base résumé—essentially one that has most of the information you'll need on it to apply for your target job, and which will simply require tweaks and adjustments for each application. So before we get to each of the letters in GLORY, first find three to five job descriptions that are representative of the job you're pursuing. All must be for the same type of job. You will read these job descriptions to see what keeps popping up across all of them regarding skills and requirements. This will help make sure your base résumé has the right information.

Clients have told me that the GLORY Formula is transformational. It not only gives them a winning résumé that lands many interviews, but it elevates their confidence and completely changes the way they talk about their accomplishments in interviews.

Those same clients also say that it is challenging. As with anything truly worth doing, be prepared to do some serious work in this chapter. The GLORY Formula helps you to identify and craft exactly what should go on your résumé. This work then becomes the basis for your online branding and job interviews.

Now, let's walk through each of the GLORY Formula steps to define your value in the market and make you irresistible to companies.

G—Gather Keywords

For the first step, Gather Keywords, you read the job descriptions you've collected and highlight the terms that are specific to the profession and can be classified as a "hard skill." Hard skills refer to specific technical or specialized knowledge and abilities that are measurable and teachable. Examples of hard skills found in job descriptions include project management, graphic design, financial analysis, and benefits administration.

The keywords you highlight do not need to always be hyperspecific to the role, but they also should not be skills that many jobs require or that could be considered a "soft skill." Soft skills are personal attributes, traits, or qualities that are not easily measurable and are more related to interpersonal and social abilities. These skills are often transferable and can contribute to a person's effectiveness in various professional settings. Examples of soft skills mentioned in job descriptions include time management, attention to detail, problem-solving, and creative thinking.

While soft skills are hugely important to be successful in jobs and are evaluated in the interview process, they should not be specifically stated on your résumé or other job search documents.

Example: Financial Analyst

SOFT SKILLS	HARD SKILLS
✘ Communication	✔ Financial modeling
✘ Critical thinking	✔ Economic analysis
✘ Problem-solving	✔ Risk management
✘ Time management	✔ Financial analysis
✘ Teamwork	✔ Regulatory compliance

Instead, we focus on keywords. Keywords allow recruiters and hiring managers to immediately see that you have the correct expertise for the role they are hiring for. Keywords are specific enough to be relevant for a small subset of jobs, so they make it clear that you are qualified.

Let's take this bullet from a description for an event coordinator job; what are the keywords?

Collaborate and communicate effectively with vendors to plan frequent conferences and fun company events.

Many people get tripped up here and think "collaborate" and "communicate" are keywords, and therefore are things that they should put on their résumé. That is incorrect.

Those are soft skills and are extremely broad. Many different types of jobs—I'd go so far as to say *most* jobs—require communication and collaboration, so by highlighting these skills on your résumé, you will come across as generic. Of course those skills are important, but instead you'll show that you have them in the *way* you describe your accomplishments.

The actual keywords from the job description here are "vendors," "conferences," and "company events."

So, as we gather our keywords, our job description would look like this:

Collaborate and communicate effectively with <u>vendors</u> to plan frequent <u>conferences</u> and fun <u>company events</u>.

These keywords are fairly specific to this type of job, and if hiring managers see these words on your résumé, they'll view you as experienced and familiar with the demands of the role.

Figuring out the hard skill keywords can be challenging, as it is a bit nuanced. But once you master this, it is a huge step toward speaking the language the companies are looking for. Seriously, this keyword exercise is the basis of your résumé, your online branding, and what you'll say in the interview. You're learning to see a job description the way recruiters and hiring managers see it.

Once you've thoroughly read and highlighted the keywords in the job descriptions you gathered, pull out only the role-specific keywords and list them in a document or notebook. These are the words and phrases that you will pack into your résumé and online presence to dramatically increase the number of companies interested in you.

L—List Tasks Performed

The next step is to List Tasks Performed. I recommend dividing a sheet of paper, digital or physical, into two columns, with the left column containing the keywords you gathered, and the right column listing out the tasks you've done for your most recent job (or project, volunteer opportunity—anything where you used skills!) that have any sort of overlap with those keywords.

KEYWORDS FOR CORPORATE EVENTS MANAGER ROLES	TASKS COMPLETED IN PAST JOB AS AN EXECUTIVE ASSISTANT
Event planning	Planned quarterly strategic planning retreats
Vendor negotiation	Negotiated with event and office vendors
Logistics coordination	Managed travel and lodging accommodations for many leaders

What we are doing here is narrowing the focus of your own experience to only what the company has specifically asked for. The mistake most people make when writing their résumé is to focus first on the tasks they do most. Forget this mindset.

> *It's not about what you do most often, it's about what's most relevant to the job you're applying for.*

For example, let's say one of the keywords on the job description is "presentation design" and you once created slides for a board meeting. You would list "designed board meeting presentation" as the task performed, even if you did it only that one time. Relevance over frequency.

If the job you want next is similar to your most recent job, this exercise should be fairly straightforward. Your biggest challenge will be simply to not rebel against this formula and sneak in some tasks that aren't actually relevant. For example, say you're going from a generalist human resources role to a specialist learning and development role focused on training employees; you may be tempted to talk about that incredible compensation analysis you did that reimagined the way the company paid people and helped the business to save money while retaining employees—but that's not what they are asking for in a learning and development role. It's going to sting to set these big, juicy accomplishments aside in the name of showing the company you are exactly the square peg for their square hole, but since it will help you land the interview, it'll be worth it.

Now, if you're a career changer, you may at first glance deem this exercise impossible.

I'm telling you that you can't add your transferable soft skills, and asking you to write down tasks you performed that are relevant to a completely different profession. It sounds like a tall order, but I help my career-changing clients do it every day. This process will actually show you how much you can offer a company in a different industry.

For example, let's say you work in customer support, but you want to become a product manager. That is a major career pivot, but I am sure there are tasks you've performed around product manager job description keywords like "user experience" and "customer data." It's incredible the overlap you can find when you focus on relevancy over frequency.

While we can word-smith our way into showing more relevant experience, there may be skill gaps that you need to fill. To make the transition to product manager, you'd likely need a certain level of proficiency in the product management life cycle. This can come from a combination of education, personal projects, freelance work, volunteer work, and shadowing or contributing to your product team at your current job.

Go through each of your past roles one by one, listing the tasks performed that fit your keywords. It is most important to do this for the last two roles you've held, as those roles will get disproportionately more attention than the rest of your experience. If one (or more) of your earlier roles has very few or no tasks that address the keywords, then you may leave that experience off your résumé entirely, or simply list it without any bullets underneath it.

Remember, the hiring team will be most focused on your two most recent roles and they are also not interested in reading a detailed and accurate account of all your previous jobs. If a job from ten years ago isn't relevant to your career path, you can note it to show you were employed, but the company does not need all the details about it. You'll notice that as you do this, it also helps make your résumé much more concise.

O—Observe Your Story

The way we diminish the value of our own work is astounding. As you Observe Your Story, you'll start to see that what you viewed as "doing what needed to be done" was also work that was highly valuable and well executed.

You may suffer from "I Just" Syndrome. This is the mentality that so many talented professionals have about their work, where, when I ask them to explain their job history, I hear comments like:

- "I just did what needed to be done—I don't know that there's any special accomplishment there."
- "I just assisted on that project, so I can't take credit."
- "I just volunteered there; that wasn't real paid work."

Yet, they "assisted" with a task that was vital to the end success of the project. And when they weren't doing "real paid work" they were actually utilizing real skills and adding real value. Nothing fake about that!

When you Observe Your Story it is the chocolate chip in the cookie—truly the part that makes this all worth it. This step transforms the way people think about their experience.

It takes a real mindset shift. And the way you currently think about your experience probably could use a bit of a transformation, if you don't mind me saying so.

Before we dive into how to Observe Your Story, I will warn you: This process also takes a lot of reflection. You may become frustrated, thinking things like:

- "This takes a while!"
- "I'm struggling to remember my past work."
- "I have so much information written down, how will I condense this into a résumé bullet?"

All of these thoughts are common and completely valid. I urge you to push past those feelings and stick with me, because on the other side of this exercise is a new perspective on your expertise.

What you'll want to do first is pick one of the tasks that you listed in the second step of the GLORY Formula, List Tasks Performed. I recommend starting with one that gives you the clearest feeling that you accomplished something, as that will make this a bit easier. You'll go through the set of questions below for that task. Then when you're done with that task, you'll pick another one on the list, until you've done enough to have several for each of your recent roles.

Here are the questions to ask yourself about each task:

- What were things like before you did this task? How much worse were things?
- What would have been the consequences of not accomplishing this?

- What was the journey to get to completing this task? How much effort did it take?
- How much of it did you control and make happen? Even if you weren't technically the leader, what aspects of it did you lead?
- What were the results?
- What was the impact of those results?

Your answers to these questions can be just a few words—though for some of them you could probably write paragraphs! Additionally, not all questions will be relevant to all tasks.

Let's walk through an example. Continuing from our example above, we choose the first task to expand on, "planned quarterly strategic planning retreats."

KEYWORDS FOR CORPORATE EVENTS MANAGER ROLES	TASKS COMPLETED IN PAST JOB AS AN EXECUTIVE ASSISTANT
Event planning	Planned quarterly strategic planning retreats

Then we follow the series of questions:

- What were things like before you did this task? How much worse were things?
  - ▶ *Quarterly planning was done in-office. It wasn't very comfortable fitting all senior managers in our conference room, and keeping everyone in the office didn't help leaders to think creatively.*

- What would have been the consequences of not accomplishing this?
  - ▶ *Continuing to be uncomfortable in the office. Potentially worse, less focused planning.*

- What was the journey to get to completing this task? How much effort did it take?
  - ▶ *Had to identify venues, find catering vendors, coordinate travel and lodging, print booklets, organize decks, and send out communications.*

- How much of it did you control and make happen? Even if you weren't technically the leader, what aspects of it did you lead?
  - ▶ *I managed all of the logistics. I had a bit of help, but for the tasks I didn't do myself I was responsible for delegating.*

- What were the results?
  - ▶ *I have organized a full year of quarterly offsites so far. Each one had many attendees from senior management. I repeatedly get feedback from attendees on how much people benefit from getting out of the office, and how well organized the offsite is.*

- What was the impact of those results?
  - ▶ *Satisfied attendees and improved strategic planning.*

Okay, see how handling the logistics of a quarterly retreat is actually a hugely important task that impacts all of senior management, which means it indirectly impacts the whole company and enhances the company's ability to strategically plan? That's huge! This is the power of Observing Your Story.

One challenge you may face is remembering your experiences. For example, how do you remember what you did eight years ago? If there are any old files, papers, social posts, or emails you can use to spark your memory, investigate those. It's understandable if you don't have access to any of those things, as most companies do their best to revoke access to those items when you leave. If there's someone on your old team you still keep in touch with, you could reach out to them and ask what *they* put on their résumé, as another way to trigger your memory.

Work on the GLORY Formula over multiple days to give your mind time away from the activity to remember. Once your mind is primed to think about your previous roles, you may find your memory being triggered by things happening in your day-to-day. For example, I saw a commercial for peanut butter the other day, and it brought me back to over a decade ago when I worked in market research and took notes on people's reactions to new peanut butter snacks. I could probably muster a résumé bullet out of my vague recollection of this work, massaging in keywords like "qualitative data" and "focus groups," if relevant to the next job I wanted.

During this step, the key is to give yourself grace. Being perfectly precise is not important. The general idea of what you did is often good enough. And if someone in an interview asks you to walk through an accomplishment in detail that happened a decade ago, kindly say, "I'll do my best, but since it was ten years ago the details are a bit fuzzy." Sometimes interviewers need this reminder. (Even better, the Job Shopper approach would be to recommend a similarly relevant example that you remember more clearly!)

It's time to Observe Your Story and obliterate "I Just" Syndrome. See the value of your actions and stop minimizing your very real contributions. Take time to move from question to question for each of your accomplishments. This will be the basis for your résumé bullets, but will also start to shape the way you talk about yourself for other job search branding and your job interviews. Do your best and be nonjudgmental about the way you describe the experience. This step is about getting the information out of your head and onto paper. All the editing will come in the next step.

R—Refine the Accomplishment

The next step in the GLORY Formula is to Refine the Accomplishment. You've answered the questions in the previous step and become clear on your story, and now it's time to create a cohesive résumé accomplishment bullet.

We first need to distinguish the difference between a responsibility and an accomplishment. The majority of résumés list responsibilities, such as:

- Responsible for negotiating with event and office vendors

I think of responsibilities as tasks or duties that you were assigned or expected to perform in a particular role or position. Responsibilities typically describe the day-to-day activities and expectations related to a specific position. The critical word here is "expectations."

On the other hand, an accomplishment highlights the

achievements, results, or contributions you have made in your past roles. Accomplishments demonstrate how effectively you performed your responsibilities and the impact you had on the organization or team. Accomplishments typically showcase your skills, abilities, and the value you brought to your previous employers. We want to fill your résumé with accomplishments rather than responsibilities.

> *The reason why responsibilities are less valuable on a résumé is because you're listing what you were expected to do, but it doesn't give any indication of whether you were good at doing it.*

I may be "responsible for" making sure I exercise every day, but that does not mean I hit anywhere close to that goal. On the other hand, if I told you that I have motivated myself to exercise for thirty minutes five days a week for six months straight, that would give you the context of what I am capable of—a real accomplishment.

So what would "responsible for negotiating with event and office vendors" look like as an accomplishment? Something like:

- Negotiated with 15+ event vendors, with some contracts exceeding $60,000, and landed discounts of 10%+ across several vendors

Using accomplishments over responsibilities makes your résumé sound impressive, and it's actually very easy to make the transformation. You just need one simple bullet formula for your entire résumé.

A great résumé accomplishment bullet has three core components:

- Action verb
- Keywords
- Quantification

ACTION VERBS

Action verbs are strong and specific words that convey a sense of achievement and highlight your active role in completing a task or achieving a goal. Examples of action verbs include:

Achieved	Implemented	Led
Resolved	Improved	Generated
Created	Initiated	Managed

KEYWORDS

Keywords are relevant terms or phrases specific to your industry or the job you are applying for. The good news is, you already collected these in the Gather Keywords step, and they were the throughline when you Listed Tasks Performed and Observed Your Story, so you should be able to easily integrate these into your résumé accomplishment. When drafting your accomplishment, know that you do not need to limit yourself to one keyword per bullet—it's likely that multiple keywords will work in your bullet, and that's excellent.

QUANTIFICATION

Quantification involves adding specific numbers, metrics, percentages, or other quantifiable measures to describe the scope and impact of your accomplishments. By including quantifiable information, you provide tangible evidence of your success and demonstrate the value you brought to your previous roles.

Here are some ways to quantify your work:

TYPE	DESCRIPTION	EXAMPLE
Money	Budget, revenue, cost	Annual budget of $200,000
Time	Length or amount	9-month-long project
Amount	People, tasks, etc.	Wrote 10+ articles
Frequency	Per day, week, month	Scheduled 40–50 meetings a week
Growth	Money, volume, percentage increase	33% increase in satisfaction
Reduction	Money, volume, percentage decrease	Streamlined process from 12 steps to 4 steps
Scale	How many? How big?	120 attendees

At a basic level, you need to start counting things about your work. Count the number of months you did something for. Count the typical volume of inquiries you addressed. Count the number of people involved. The number doesn't need to be super big, or even super accurate. Use estimations when needed.

CREATING YOUR ACCOMPLISHMENT BULLET

By incorporating these three components into your accomplishment bullets, you create strong, impactful statements that effectively communicate your achievements, highlight your skills, and differentiate you from other candidates. You'll want to be specific, concise, and results-oriented when crafting your accomplishment statements.

Following our example, we identified the keyword "event planning," listed the task performed as "planned quarterly strategic planning retreats," and uncovered in observing our story that we satisfied attendees and improved strategic planning.

Now we need to come up with the action verb to begin crafting our bullet. How about "managed"? You did manage the event logistics, after all. So here is our keyword and our action verb in a bullet:

- **Managed** the **event planning** of quarterly retreats, resulting in high satisfaction from attendees and improved strategic planning

Finally, it's time to quantify the accomplishment. So many people tell me, "Madeline, I can't quantify my work experience!" But that simply is not true. Your work can be quantified, full stop.

Looking at our bullet, the first and easiest thing to do is count: How many retreats did you plan? And approximately how many attendees were there?

- Managed the event planning of **4** quarterly retreats with ***100+ attendees***, resulting in high satisfaction from attendees and improved strategic planning

Notice I put "100+ attendees." Having an exact number here isn't important. What's most important is to have a fair estimate so that the reader can understand the *scale* of what you did. An event for 10 people is a different accomplishment than an event for 100 people, which is different than for 1,000 people. But the difference between 100 and 120 attendees is negligible. And when you make a conservative estimate and then put a "+" after it, it is always accurate.

Now let's quantify the second half. It's common practice to send out a feedback form after an event. So let's say you sent out a short survey and one of the questions was to rate the satisfaction of the event on a scale from 1 to 10. You categorize answers that are 8 through 10 as "satisfied" and answers of 1 through 7 as "unsatisfied." You calculate the percentage of respondents who gave an 8 or above score and find that it is 93 percent. This brings our bullet to:

- Managed the event planning of **4** quarterly retreats with ***100+ attendees***, resulting in a ***93% satisfaction score*** from attendees and improved strategic planning

To create effective bullets on your résumé, be sure to shift your focus away from responsibilities and toward accomplishments. Craft each accomplishment with an action verb to convey a sense of achievement and emphasize your active role. Incorporate the role-specific keywords that you identified in the first two steps of the GLORY Formula. Finally, quantify your accomplishments by including specific numbers, metrics, or percentages. This adds credibility and provides tangible evidence of your success. By combining these three components, you can create concise and compelling accomplishment statements that showcase your achievements, skills, and value to potential employers.

Y—Yes Statements

I am happy to say at this point that you have done all of the hard work. Now it's time to sprinkle on Yes Statements. These are statements placed in a highlights section at the top of your résumé—or alternatively in your experience section—that allow a hiring manager to skim the paper in thirty seconds and understand why they should hire you. Yes Statements will be tailored specifically to the role you've applied to; they are the ones that will make the hiring manager put your résumé in the "yes" pile to move forward in the process.

Yes Statements are placed in your résumé for several reasons:

- To draw attention to specific expertise that may not be found easily on your résumé

- To focus on accomplishments that are from several jobs ago but relevant to the opportunity you're applying for
- To translate how a past role actually had you perform tasks relevant to your target role

This is all to say: If you are clearly qualified for your next role (because you have the same or a similar job title, or one that is one step down), then you don't need Yes Statements. However, if you're making a career pivot, or your best experience is from a few jobs ago, Yes Statements and a highlights section are going to be helpful.

CREATING YOUR YES STATEMENTS

Yes Statements are important if your most recent role isn't exactly in line with your next opportunity. So if you are a front-end software engineer now going for senior front-end software engineer, you won't rely on Yes Statements as much as if you are a front-end software engineer applying for a project manager role. It's also common that you may have experience relevant to the role you're interested in, but that experience happened several jobs ago and therefore isn't at the top of your résumé. That makes Yes Statements at the start of your résumé all the more important.

Yes Statements are simple. They are essentially summaries that call out important keywords so that the person reading your résumé quickly understands that you have the correct skills and knowledge. This can look like a bullet at the top of the résumé in a highlights or summary section that says:

_____ professional with experience in _____, _____, and _____ in the _____ industry

The first blank helps to translate the type of professional you are. If you are a front-end software engineer who has taken project management courses and done project management work, even if it was informally and without the title, you can still say you are a "project management professional." A professional is someone who has the skills and knowledge to do a job, so claim it. Another way to do this is to find the commonality between your current job and the next job. So an overlap between being a front-end software engineer and a project manager could be a "technology professional" or a "software professional."

The next three blanks are for keywords for the role, so that we are right up top telling the reader, "I have the skills you're looking for, don't worry!" Typically you'll choose the top three keywords that you identified in the Gather Keywords stage. A top keyword is one that is used often and/or is at the top of job descriptions, usually either in the summary paragraph at the top or in the first three bullets of the job description.

In this situation, this Yes Statement could read:

- Software professional with experience in project management, technical documentation, and the software development life cycle

Then include the industry only if it's in line with the role you're interested in. If not, then leave the industry out.

Now your bullet reads:

- Software professional with experience in project management, technical documentation, and the software development life cycle in the **technology industry**

This template is highly effective, but you can also add some bells and whistles to it by including accomplishments here, or adjusting the wording. Make the formula work for your situation.

As I mentioned earlier, one great place to put your Yes Statements is in a highlights section at the top of your résumé, especially if your most relevant job experience is not from your most recent job. A highlights section is exactly what it sounds like: a small section at the top of your résumé

Résumé

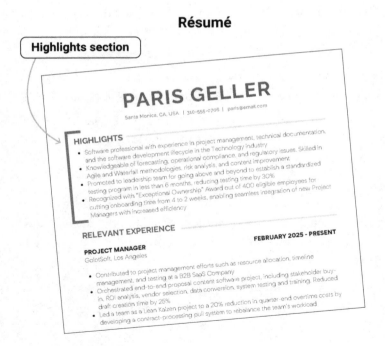

Highlights section

PARIS GELLER

Santa Monica, CA, USA | 310-555-0706 | paris@email.com

HIGHLIGHTS
- Software professional with experience in project management, technical documentation, and the software development lifecycle in the Technology industry
- Knowledgeable of forecasting, operational compliance, and regulatory issues. Skilled in Agile and Waterfall methodologies, risk analysis, and content improvement
- Promoted to leadership team for going above and beyond to establish a standardized testing program in less than 6 months, reducing testing time by 30%
- Recognized with "Exceptional Ownership" Award out of 400 eligible employees for cutting onboarding time from 4 to 2 weeks, enabling seamless integration of new Project Managers with increased efficiency

RELEVANT EXPERIENCE

PROJECT MANAGER   FEBRUARY 2025 - PRESENT
GolotSoft, Los Angeles
- Contributed to project management efforts such as resource allocation, timeline management, and testing at a B2B SaaS Company
- Orchestrated end-to-end proposal content software project, including stakeholder buy-in, ROI analysis, vendor selection, data conversion, system testing and training. Reduced draft creation time by 25%
- Led a team as a Lean Kaizen project to a 20% reduction in quarter-end overtime costs by developing a contract-processing pull system to rebalance the team's workload

containing your incredible Yes Statements and other notable information for the résumé reader.

Once you have your Yes Statements in the highlights section, you can then fill in the rest of the section by noting important certifications you have and the most relevant accomplishments from your past. Essentially, you want to write the highlights section in such a way that even if the reader doesn't go beyond that first section, they will already know you're qualified.

While Yes Statements are typically in a highlights section, you can instead put Yes Statements at the top of your experience section. At the top of each job experience, you can give a brief summary of what important tasks you performed at that role that fulfill the keywords, sounding something like:

Résumé

PARIS GELLER

Santa Monica, CA, USA | 310-555-0706 | paris@email.com

HIGHLIGHTS
- Software professional with experience in project management, technical documentation, and the software development lifecycle in the Technology industry
- Knowledgeable of forecasting, operational compliance, and regulatory issues. Skilled in Agile and Waterfall methodologies, risk analysis, and content improvement
- Promoted to leadership team for going above and beyond to establish a standardized testing program in less than 6 months, reducing testing time by 30%
- Recognized with "Exceptional Ownership" Award out of 400 eligible employees for cutting onboarding time from 4 to 2 weeks, enabling seamless integration of new Project Managers with increased efficiency

RELEVANT EXPERIENCE

PROJECT MANAGER   FEBRUARY 2025 - PRESENT
GolotSoft, Los Angeles

- Contributed to project management efforts such as resource allocation, timeline management, and testing at a B2B SaaS Company
- [covered] end-to-end proposal of current software project, including stakeholder buy-in, ROI analysis, vendor selection, data conversion, system testing and training. Reduced draft creation time by 25%
- Led a team as a Lean Kaizen project to a 20% reduction in quarter-end overtime costs by developing a contract-processing pull system to rebalance the team's workload

Yes Statement

> Contributed to project management efforts such as re-source allocation, timeline management, and testing at a B2B SaaS company

After this Yes Statement you can dive into the actual accomplishments, but, like a highlights section, this hits them right up top with a clear summary of what you did at this job that was relevant, and the type of company it was.

My motto when creating résumés is that you should use approaches that serve you and skip ones that don't. As much as I want to pop a telescope out of this book and peer into your résumé to give you customized feedback, I can't! Therefore it's important to not forget the core mission here: give the company recruiters the information they need to quickly see that you can do the job they're hiring for. When creating a résumé, it's not about following the "rules" of what a résumé should be. I still recommend following the regular formatting conventions for résumés, because the predictability makes for an effortless reading experience for the reader. But the trick for Job Shoppers is the way we craft the actual information: our goal must be to provide the reader with only the most relevant details, and to make it as clear as possible, as quickly as possible, that you are the right person for the job.

Follow the GLORY Formula so that you start with the company's needs in mind first, and then build your result around those keywords. Not because you're terrified some résumé-scanning robot is going to put your application in job app purgatory, but because *people* are looking for these keywords.

Find tasks that overlap with what the company is looking for and observe the value you brought to those tasks. Condense those accomplishments into nice neat résumé bullets, and then add Yes Statements at the top of or throughout your résumé, wherever you need to center the reader's attention on important skills and experiences.

My clients say that their GLORY Formula résumés are the best-performing résumés they have ever had, not because they have some new fancy formatting but because the content is so dang compelling. The hiring manager reads it and immediately sees the connection between your skill set and the role they are trying to fill. This is the secret to finding the glory in your story.

Key Takeaways

- Tailor your application materials to highlight how you can fulfill the company's needs, rather than focusing on your own story or including every detail of your career history on your résumé.

- Follow the GLORY Formula (Gather Keywords, List Tasks Performed, Observe Your Story, Refine the Accomplishment, Yes Statements) to create a targeted and effective résumé that resonates with hiring managers.

- Gather Keywords: Find specific hard skills mentioned in job descriptions.

- List Tasks Performed: Identify what you've done in previous jobs that match the hard skills the job descriptions demand.

- Observe Your Story: Recognize the value and impact of your past experiences by reflecting on the tasks you've performed, the challenges you've overcome, and the results you've achieved.

- Refine the Accomplishment: Craft each résumé accomplishment with the following elements: Action Verb + Keywords + Quantification.

- Yes Statements: Place these lines strategically at the top of your résumé or within experience sections to highlight relevant skills, experience, and accomplishments tailored to the job you're applying for.

Chapter 5

BUILD YOUR BRAND AND THE JOBS WILL FIND YOU

The year is 1992. You open the phone book to the first page. The first entry you see is A & A Mortgage Co. of Westlake Village. What does A & A stand for? Possibly two business partners, Adams and Anderson? Or maybe descriptors like American and Articulate? No, it turns out A & A stands for nothing; it was simply a ploy to get the coveted first spot in the yellow pages . . . and it worked.

Of course, these days companies have gone digital and focus on search engine optimization. But back in the day, when phone books were categorized alphabetically, businesses had ridiculous company names, such as the grammatically questionable A Accurate Telephone Answering Service, A Ace Pest & Termite Control, and A Action Key Safe & Locksmith's, in order to be the first company that potential clients would see when they flipped open the pages. One thing business owners understand is that you can have the best service in town, but if people don't know you exist, it's a moot point, like throwing a party and forgetting to send out the invites.

When a person has a need, businesses know it's important to be easily findable, so they can be the one to address that need. It's not about being the best option in the industry, but instead the best option people can easily find. The same is true for you when it comes to hiring.

When a company has an open role, *you* should be the person who shows up in their search.

> **The secret to always having a job: you don't have to be the most talented person in your industry, you just have to be the most easily found.**

Companies with skilled roles to fill will often hire recruiters, sourcers, and headhunters to find the talent they are looking for. These professionals actively search for candidates who possess the desired skills and qualifications for specific roles. They use their networks, online platforms, and databases to identify potential candidates and connect them with the hiring company. This is how they help companies increase their chances of finding suitable candidates and filling their open positions quickly.

But if you're not easily findable online, how are these recruiters supposed to reach out to you? If you're not currently easy to find online, with the help of this chapter we're going to fix that and make you inescapable!

Imagine what it would feel like if your dream company reached out to you directly, asking if you were interested in a role. This is the reality for my clients. Many of them can stop applying online and instead get regular messages from recruiters inviting them to interview with companies. And it's all from building an online brand. In this chapter you'll learn how to be more easily found so that job opportunities come to you.

Why Do Companies Source Talent?

One afternoon I received an email from a recruiter representing a renewable energy company that I had never heard of. He said they were looking for another human resources leader to join the team, and according to what he saw on my LinkedIn profile, I fit the bill. I was happy with my job and didn't have this company on my "dream employer" list, but I decided to take the call as an opportunity to network with the recruiter.

I was honest with him on the call that I wasn't particularly interested in leaving my job, but I still answered his questions about my background. He encouraged me to meet with the VP of People at the company since he thought we would get along well, and if there didn't seem to be a fit with working together, no problem.

Well, this VP was phenomenal. She was a visionary thinker, highly strategic, and she was even coaching me on the call about my next career move. I adored her, and when they invited me to further interviews, again I thought, "Couldn't hurt!"

Several rounds of interviews later I had an offer in hand and was seriously considering working with them after never dreaming it would get to this stage! After careful consideration of my career goals and job needs, I decided to take the plunge with this renewable energy company that had been a complete unknown to me just a few weeks earlier.

In a landscape where job postings attract hundreds of applications, how does sourcing make sense? Think about it—when a company needs top-notch talent, they're not content to sit back and wait for the perfect résumé to magically land in their inbox.

When you realize the benefits of sourcing, it is clear why so many companies do it. First, certain roles may require specialized skills or qualifications that are in high demand or limited supply. In such cases, waiting until you get the right applications may not yield enough qualified candidates. Sourcing enables companies to proactively search for individuals with specific experience and attract them to consider the job openings.

Moreover, sourcing can help companies gain a competitive advantage in the hiring process. In today's cutthroat job market, top talent is often in high demand and may receive multiple job offers. By engaging in sourcing, companies can reach out to potential candidates before they have a chance to apply elsewhere, increasing the likelihood of securing highly qualified individuals. Sourcing allows companies to be proactive and assertive in their recruitment efforts, which can be particularly beneficial for filling critical or hard-to-fill positions.

By continuously searching for and engaging with potential candidates, companies can create a pool of interested individuals they can consider for future job openings. This approach helps streamline the hiring process and reduces the time and effort required to fill positions when the need arises.

Many companies believe that in order to get the top talent in the industry, they may need to steal them from other companies. You want someone who is a happy, productive high performer to come work for you, and unfortunately, a lot of those people already have jobs. So as a company you can either sit and hope those top performers decide they want to go through the bother of filling out an online application, or you can be proactive and reach out to them. Hiring is such a crucial part of a company's success that many of them don't like to hire passively, but actively seek out the perfect candidate.

Your goal, then, is to be the candidate that they find. Have those qualifications that they are searching for. Be the candidate they think of when a role in your field is open. In order to be sourced, you don't have to be employed, you don't have to know people at the company, and you don't even have to have worked in the field before. It's all about positioning yourself properly online to have the opportunities flow to you.

Building Your Online Brand to Get Sourced

Tara was a graphic designer who felt like daily interactions at her toxic workplace left her trying to navigate a minefield . . . in stilettos. Every week on our coaching calls, she'd show up like a weary soldier returning from battle, recounting tales of her boss's relentless onslaught of impossible deadlines and soul-crushing critiques.

Tara knew she had to leave this job, but her confidence was at an all-time low, and she struggled to land interviews. When she did, she wasn't able to make it past the first two rounds.

Everything changed when Tara was coached on getting clarity in her career. She realized she wanted to pivot to being a user experience designer, and already was doing a good bit of UX work in her current position. With a clear target in mind, Tara took to heart every LinkedIn profile edit I suggested. She also used my recommended networking strategy to grow her LinkedIn connections from ninety-two people when we met to over a thousand by the time she landed her next job. These changes—culminating in the targeted creation of a personal brand—took Tara from zero recruiter outreaches to fifteen recruiters a week.

Tara was quickly attracting the right types of opportunities and became an in-demand Job Shopper. She not only landed a new role, but afterward continued to get recruiter outreaches asking her to interview, firmly shifting her mentality to the knowledge that she never again has to "tough it out" with a toxic employer for a paycheck.

So how did Tara do it? With a strong online brand. While there are countless places and websites where a professional may be found, none has had quite the stronghold on recruiter sourcing as LinkedIn.

Note: It's worth it to create a LinkedIn profile no matter what industry you are in, but do note that the most common jobs recruiters search for on LinkedIn are corporate "desk jobs," while those in education, skilled trades, and retail, to name a few, are less common. This is important, because while you can follow Tara's approach to a T on LinkedIn, you'll never show up in recruiter searches if no recruiters are searching for that role.

Now, let's start elevating your online brand!

Step 1: Focus Your Profile around the Job You Hope to Get

We want to think about our online branding like a sign for a storefront. We wouldn't say "Open to New Customers," nor would we say "Aspiring Arts and Crafts Store." No, on the sign we would simply claim what we sell in the store, before the first customer has ever bought from us.

The same is true for your online personal branding. Too many people put in the LinkedIn headlines "Open to Opportunities," as if this is the phrase that will have companies flocking to your page. Instead, you need to focus on what you're offering. If it's something that a company is looking for, that is going to lead to more opportunities.

It's also important that you focus all your online branding around the value you will add, not where you have been. For example, it's counterproductive to say things like "Former Teacher Who Is an Aspiring Graphic Designer," or "Military Veteran Looking to Become a Sales Representative." Instead, build the skills of a graphic designer, and call yourself a graphic designer. Take a sales course, and then brand yourself a sales professional. When you are clear on exactly what job you want next, not where you have been, companies will be much more likely to approach you with opportunities.

So what does the ideal profile look like? At the top, the headline clearly states your target profession and industry. All work samples and summaries about your work history should revolve around this chosen profession. We don't need four paragraphs on all the twists and turns your career took to get you to where you are. Instead we want to know where your career is going, why you are excited about it, and what experience from your past sets you up perfectly to succeed in it.

Take a moment now to review your online presence. Look at any professional networking websites you're on, your portfolio website, and anywhere else that makes up your professional online brand. As you land on each of those pages, is it immediately clear what job a company should hire you for?

Finally, check your privacy settings online. For any networking site that you're on, your profile's privacy settings should be completely public. If your profile is on lockdown that's tighter than Fort Knox, you're missing out on opportunities. Too many people accidentally leave their privacy settings configured in such a way that their photo, last name, or sometimes even full profile cannot be viewed without the visitor sending a connection request and having it accepted. This automatically suppresses the amount of opportunities you will get. Just like a local business would never make its website private, or password-protected, you shouldn't do that with your professional profiles either.

Step 2: Put the Right Keywords on Your Profile

The most important part to your branding and being easily found online by recruiters and sourcers is having the right keywords associated with your expertise.

There are several different things that recruiters typically search for. The first is job titles. They are looking for people who have job titles similar or related to the role they are hiring for. Knowing this, review your past few job titles. One tricky thing about job titles is that companies use different terms to define the same type of job.

> *It is helpful to recruiters and people outside of your current company if you "translate" your internal job title to be something more accurate or recognizable.*

Let's say that your role is called Administrative Coordinator. You look online and see that your duties are nearly identical to Project Manager roles. It would be helpful to translate your experience on LinkedIn to show your title as "Project Manager (Administrative Coordinator)."

Another example is your company may call all writers Contributors, when that doesn't reflect your expertise. You want to attract more recruiters who will provide you with entertainment-focused opportunities, so instead on LinkedIn you may put as your most recent role "Contributor—Film and Television Critic."

The second thing that recruiters search for are skills and keywords associated with the profession. All of that work you did for the Gather Keywords step of the GLORY Formula is once again going to come in handy. You'll want to focus on the top five keywords you narrowed down to in the last chapter, as well as look for keywords that frequently show up in the titles of the jobs you want. By combining your previous top five keywords with the title keywords, you can create a new top five keyword list for your LinkedIn page.

Places to put several of these keywords are at the top of your LinkedIn profile, résumé, and personal website. A data analyst may say:

> *Data Analyst | SQL | Tableau | Data Visualization | Business Analytics*

To break this down for you, the first phrase, "data analyst," is the job title the person is targeting, and then the next four keywords are skills and terms associated with the role. These keywords are specific enough to the data analysis profession that, should a search be done, this person has increased their likelihood of being found.

Then when it comes to other parts of your profile and websites, you can start to look beyond your top five keywords list a bit and add additional keywords to your personal branding when providing summaries of your career, describing your experience, and listing skills. To get an understanding of what recruiters search for versus don't search for, here are some examples:

If a recruiter was looking to hire a human resources professional, they would *not* run a search with words like "communicate," "team," or "collaborative." These terms, while relevant to the human resources role, do not identify the skill set that is unique to the human resources profession. Typing these things in would not help a recruiter find a highly skilled human resources leader.

So what would help a recruiter find a human resources professional to hire? Well, let's start with words found commonly in human resources titles: "human resources," "people operations," "talent," and "recruiting." If you were pursuing a human resources role, you would want most of these keywords on your profile. Then, you would want to sprinkle human resources–specific skills throughout your profile as well, such as "onboarding," "employee relations," "benefits enrollment," and so on. These are a few of the many more specific words that need to be on your profile.

Keywords for a Human Resources Role

NOT A KEYWORD	A KEYWORD
Communicate	Human resources
Team	Onboarding
Collaboration	Employee relations

We are focused on the keywords pertaining to your role, but I'll give you bonus points for having industry-specific keywords connected to your online presence. For example, if you indicate that you work for medical device companies, fine arts museums, or Software as a Service startups, you're giving great specificity on the kind of industry you want to be in.

Being clear about the type of company and industry you are targeting will attract more opportunities. We often think that declaring these may close off opportunities, but it actually draws in more opportunities, because you appear as a perfect fit to employers in that industry.

Adjust your online presence now to have the right keywords and targeting for your desired job. If the next job you want is simply the next step up from the role you have now, focus on using the keywords of your current role. But if you are career pivoting, then focus on the role you want in the future, not the roles you've had in the past.

Step 3: Grow Your Network

I was once training a new recruiter on how to source talent for a product manager role we were hiring for. With our laptops set up next to each other, we conducted the same search on LinkedIn for talent. On my screen was a cornucopia of hundreds of pages of quality candidates. On his, a barren wasteland—we even watched a tumbleweed roll across his screen. I'm being dramatic, but the question was, why did our searches yield such different results? The answer: our professional network sizes.

LinkedIn was founded on the idea of professional *networks*. It is designed to be a place where we can connect with our professional acquaintances, and then see who they know, in order to get additional introductions. You see, LinkedIn operates on the principle of degrees of separation—if you're not connected to enough people, you might as well be lost in the Bermuda Triangle of job searches. The new recruiter who I was training had around two hundred LinkedIn connections, making his search pool dramatically smaller than mine.

This insight is incredibly important for you, because if you are not connected to enough people on LinkedIn, you will not show up in many searches. You don't have to be a first-degree connection of recruiters to be found, but you need to be connected to enough people to where you would land as a second- or third-degree connection. Having a wide pool of connections is a key component of online branding.

Therefore, if you have fewer than five hundred LinkedIn connections right now, I encourage you to focus on increasing that number. If you are a decade or more into your career, I'd expect your connections to be upwards of two thousand.

Here are several ways to increase your number of connections quickly. First, make a list of all the organizations you have been a part of (these could be philanthropies, pickup sports games, institutions of higher learning, and so on). If you can either recall or find a list of people you have met there, start to look for them on LinkedIn and connect with them. Sure, you may not have met them in a professional setting, but odds are they either have a job or know people with jobs, so it's certainly worth connecting to them. If they may not remember you, send a quick connection message stating where you met, or the mutual organization you are a part of. Otherwise, if they know you, shoot that connection request off without context. Additionally, consider the places you've worked and connect with those folks. This includes all the vendors and contractors you've worked with as well—such as the people you interfaced with at the PR firm your company hired, and the facilitator at the team offsite, anyone and everyone!

Now that you have a solid network of people who have met you or have something in common with you, it's time to add strangers into the mix. Don't worry, adding people on LinkedIn who you don't already know is normal. I recommend going on an adding spree, where you use LinkedIn search to find people in your industry and/or field and click connect on a bunch of them. If your headline shows that you are clearly in the same industry or field as the people you are connecting with, you're likely to get connections back. If there is someone who you would particularly like to connect with, I recommend adding a connection message that is customized to them. Focus on why you would like to connect and what you noticed about them, and do not ask for anything in that initial connection message. Otherwise, leave the connection message blank and let them rip. You'll often be surprised at how many people are willing to connect.

Bonus—Step 4: Create Content

Content creation is an advanced career strategy that will set your career on fire (in the best possible way). While we can sit and wait for companies to hopefully stumble across us online, it's incredibly powerful to instead build a personal brand with content creation. Creating content and building thought leadership are the closest things you'll get to putting an insurance policy on your career.

Now that you have your own landing page to the world, be that a LinkedIn profile, a personal website, or other platforms where you exist professionally, start using your voice. Create posts, write articles, be on podcasts. If you have imposter syndrome, thinking, "I'm no expert, who is going to want to hear what I have to say?" here are several ways to get started.

First, start commenting on the work of other individuals in your industry. But don't leave simple comments like "Great insight!" Instead, share what you took away from it, as well as other observations you have. Quality comments like this will get the attention of both the poster and others in your industry. Next, if you're creating your own content on a platform, it doesn't always have to be your original insights. You can summarize an article you read, or contact people in your industry to contribute to a post you're writing. For example, you could email someone in your industry with a simple message like:

Hi Evelyn,

Quick question: What is your favorite app? I am asking Product Managers what their favorite apps are and why, and compiling a post. I'd love to include you in it! Let me know, I am getting all the responses by tomorrow at 4pm PST.

This is a fun question for Evelyn to quickly answer, and you now have a reason to speak with Evelyn that isn't asking her for a job. This interaction is a one-two punch: you're building thought leadership and a relationship!

The magic of putting out content is that you are reminding people that you exist. When I first started posting professional content on social media, I didn't get much response, but then I would go to networking events and people would say things like, "I see you online a lot." So even when I didn't have a well-crafted social media strategy, people were reminded that I was in their network, and they were more likely to think of me for opportunities. Once I uncovered what I came to call the "5 Viral Triggers on LinkedIn," my engagement took off like a rocket. (If you're interested in learning more about these Triggers, visit the supplemental web page for this book at reversethesearch.com/resources.)

It's also incredible what happened when I built my personal brand in earnest: I never had to cold-message anyone again. Posting regularly made me familiar to people I had never met before. I was then able to reach out to people I had not spoken to before and they would greet me warmly: "Hey, Madeline, great to hear from you! I love your posts." This has dramatically reduced my social anxiety!

This strategy is essentially mass networking. You're building relationships at scale. It's challenging to start, but once you get the hang of it, it's incredibly rewarding and impactful. It's like planting seeds in a digital garden—eventually, you'll reap opportunities to harvest.

Here's one more personal branding tip I'll leave you with: invest in a good headshot and then use it for all platforms. If you go anywhere I exist online, you'll see that my thumbnail is the same for every account. That's not laziness, that's branding. In the digital age, we can go months or even years knowing someone mostly based on their photo. Your thumbnail is your logo, it's your golden arches. It should be immediately recognizable as you pop up on different platforms that it's you.

So take some time to work on your online presence. Make it easy to be found. The people who get the most job offers are not necessarily the ones who have the best skills or most impressive résumé; they are the ones who are easily discoverable and have a solid online brand.

Key Takeaways

- Craft your online profile, particularly on LinkedIn, to clearly reflect your target profession and industry, focusing on the value you offer rather than where you've been.

- Use the right keywords associated with your expertise throughout your profile to increase your chances of being found by recruiters and sourcers.

- Grow your professional network on LinkedIn to expand your reach and visibility, aiming for at least 500 connections, or ideally more than 2,000 for seasoned professionals.

- Consider content creation as a powerful tool to enhance your online presence and thought leadership, engaging with industry peers and showcasing your expertise.

Chapter 6

NETWORK AS
THE SHORTCUT

A colleague of mine advised me to apply to ten jobs a day, but I've been focused on doing more and getting to twenty," my client Todd said. He then scrolled through his spreadsheet of all the jobs he had applied for—hundreds of applications, with no interviews. What at first was supposed to be a document to stay organized and track progress, he had now dubbed "a doom list of rejections."

Todd had applied to over three hundred jobs and was putting in full forty-hour weeks completely committed to the job search. When he became my client, he had left his job as a music teacher two months prior. He had put in fifteen years of seventy-hour workweeks, low pay, and his full dedication. When his family faced unexpected hard times, he assumed his employer and coworkers would be there for him, but they massively let him down in his time of need.

This triggered a desire to make a career change to become a scrum master.

When he became my client, we completely shifted his job search approach, and it comes down to one idea:

Measure your progress in interactions, not applications.

Todd completely stopped applying online. Instead he took to working on himself (upskilling, rebranding his skill set, getting clear on exactly what role he wanted next) and building relationships. He had very few connections in the industries he was interested in, but did thoughtful outreaches to people he didn't know, as well as harnessing the power of "weak ties" to activate his network (which we will dive more into later). He ultimately landed two job offers, neither of which was from applying online. Instead, one was from striking up a conversation with someone at a target company, and the other was from connecting with one of his wife's friends, which ultimately led to getting a job interview.

The offer that Todd accepted was more than twice what he was making as a teacher. Additionally, his workweek went from seventy hours to less than forty hours, allowing him to spend more time with his four children and to be able to afford to take them all on vacation.

Todd took a hopeless situation of endless online applications and transformed it into one of the best decisions of his life. I tell you this because I am mildly begging you here: please trust me when I ask you to network! Your happiness is on the other side of relationship building. I promise you that it's not as bad as it seems and will absolutely transform your job search.

> *Because the bottom line is: Applying online is the slow way. Networking is the fast way.*

If Todd's situation has taught you anything, it's to banish that feeling of satisfaction you get from hitting submit on a job application. Too many of us feel that applications are the measure of productivity in the job search, when really we are simply putting our information in a database, with no guarantee that anyone will ever read it. It's like buying raffle tickets and hoping you'll win as a strategy to pay your rent that month.

Therefore, we need to measure our progress in interactions:

- How many people have you talked to this week at your target companies?
- How many people in your network have you told that you are job searching?
- How many conversations with acquaintances and friends have you had in which you casually brought up your professional interests to see if they know anyone?

The more you log these types of interactions, the faster you will land your next position. In addition, you can still apply online, but after you apply, you're not done. Every job application needs to be accompanied by an effort to get in touch with someone at the business. This could be sending an email to the hiring manager expressing your excitement and interest in the position, alerting the recruiter that your application has been submitted, or getting in touch with the person who posted about the role on their social media.

However, as you move up in your career beyond the entry level stages, it's best to focus less on submitting applications and more on being sure that other people submit the application for you. This is called being *referred*, which is the ultimate goal of all our networking. Next to being sourced, as we talked about in the last chapter, this is the best way to land an interview.

> *If you're looking for the secret to having constant opportunities in your life, in one way or another, it's networking.*

Networking allows you to have a better chance of getting sourced online or of someone referring you to a job. As discussed in the previous chapter, you can even network at scale by building an online presence. This chapter will explore how to meet people, how to network, how to get referred, and when all else fails, how to apply online and still log an interaction.

Why Do We Hate Networking So Much?

A few years back, I almost entirely stopped posting content about networking on social media. Networking is for sure the best and easiest way to land a job, but people simply wouldn't watch it. Why?

Because job seekers *hate* networking.

They don't want to do it, they don't want to learn how to

do it, and there's no sense in making social media content that people shut off immediately.

But you're here with me now. You're not swiping away. So let's get into it.

Despite networking being a clear fast route to our next job, we tend to avoid networking the same way we pretend to be engrossed in our phone to dodge making eye contact with someone trying to sell us something on the street. It's because the idea of networking makes us incredibly un-comfy.

The number one objection I hear when people talk about dreading networking is that it feels *inauthentic*. We don't want to feel like we are bothering people. It also feels incredibly vulnerable—what do we say? How do we not embarrass ourselves?

Another reason why people might find networking intimidating is because they have a misconception of what networking is and think it is only about exchanging business cards and asking for jobs directly. However, that is not the case; networking can be much more subtle and informal.

Because the fact is, whether you mean to or not, you are networking all the time. It's simply relationship building, and if that person you're talking to is employed or knows another person who is employed (so essentially everyone fits into this category), well, you could consider that networking. I had one client sheepishly say, "The only people I really talk to are at church—does that count as networking?" Absolutely! We often mistake networking as needing to speak with someone at the company we want to work for to get them to give us a job. But networking is so much broader than that. You'd be surprised how striking up a conversation with someone in line at the coffee shop can lead to you mentioning you work in customer service in the banking industry, which leads to your new acquaintance saying that their cousin's wife works at Wells Fargo, and they can put you in touch.

This is one example of how the weak ties in your life are most likely to be the ones that will land you the job interviews. The term "weak ties" was popularized by sociologist Mark Granovetter in his influential 1973 paper titled "The Strength of Weak Ties."[*] Strong ties refer to close friends and family members, while weak ties refer to acquaintances and casual contacts. Granovetter conducted a study on job-seeking behavior and found that individuals were more likely to find job opportunities through their weak ties rather than their strong ties.

Granovetter argued that weak ties are valuable in accessing new information and resources because they provide connections to different social circles and networks that might not overlap with one's own. Strong ties tend to move within the same social circles, so they are less likely to expose individuals to novel opportunities.

Regarding networking to land a job, the concept of weak ties emphasizes the importance of building and maintaining a diverse network of acquaintances and contacts. While close friends and family members are essential for support and emotional connections, they might not be as effective in help-

---

[*] Mark S. Granovetter, "The Strength of Weak Ties," *American Journal of Sociology* 78, no. 6 (May 1973): 1360–80, https://snap.stanford.edu/class /cs224w-readings/granovetter73weakties.pdf.

ing you find job opportunities outside of your immediate circle.

This does unfortunately mean that you will be more likely to land your next interview through someone you don't know very well, but that doesn't have to intimidate you. In fact, it's incredibly normal and expected.

An example of natural networking includes socializing with people at a meetup event in your area. As you talk, you realize that you have a lot in common, including your interests and experiences. You exchange contact information and agree to grab coffee sometime in the future.

Another example is you join a virtual professional organization related to your field and attend webinars and interact with the online group. You chat with people there and get to know them and their experiences.

Or, you follow and interact with people in your industry on social media platforms. As you engage with their content and participate in online discussions, you build relationships with these people. Soon, you find yourself direct-messaging them and having casual conversations about your careers, industry trends, and more.

As you engage with people, be it in person or online, don't feel like you are bothering people. In this chapter, we will walk through the most effective ways to engage in networking conversations. But if you follow those steps and people still don't help you or respond, that's normal. Don't take it personally.

When I asked people why they may not *respond* to networking messages from other professionals, some answers I received were:

- "I am not sure that I have anything helpful to offer them."
- "I wasn't really sure what they were asking for, and didn't think I was the right person."
- "I am so busy, I honestly lost track of their email, but I did intend to respond!"

When people don't respond, it's often because they're busy, or they're worried that they can't help if they engage with you, not because of anything you did or said.

On the flip side, here are the thoughts that often stop us from reaching out to someone in our industry:

- "Are they going to judge me for being a 'taker'?"
- "What could I possibly offer them in return for their help?"
- "Are they going to get annoyed at me?"

These worries are completely normal to have, and there are ways to overcome them. First, before reaching out to anyone, you'll want to keep in mind that every interaction you have with people should have pure intentions. Never expect a job or a referral, or really for them to ever do anything for you. Instead, go into the interaction with curiosity to learn about this person. Get to know what's interesting about them, what their career has been like, and what matters to them (professional or otherwise). We will discuss this more later in this chapter, but using my 60 Seconds of Value approach you'll find small ways to add value to people. If you enter into every conversation with curiosity, gratitude, and an eye for finding ways to add value to the person, you'll be surprised at how much good fortune comes right back your way.

Second, recognize that people like to talk about themselves and help others. The person you're talking to won't judge you or get annoyed at you if you allow them to do both. The key here is to give folks the feeling of the payoff of helping others. If they spend twenty-five minutes on a phone call telling you their career story and then giving you some nuggets of advice on your next career move, they better see a thank-you email in their inbox the next morning, and then another email several weeks later where you share how you've been putting their advice into action. It may sound silly, but those actions you take are essential to that person feeling good about the interaction. When someone helps another person, they are now invested in that person's story, and the kind thing to do is to shower them with gratitude and updates.

And finally, the good news is, if they don't want to help

Timeline of a Networking Call

you, they won't. It's as simple as that. You asking for help and someone not responding is the same as never asking at all. You're at the same spot you were before you asked, but at least you gave it a shot. Don't add meaning to the interaction beyond that.

We often overthink networking and it paralyzes us. In this chapter we will learn how to shake that inaction. It is important to remember that networking is not just about finding a job, it is also about building professional relationships and expanding your knowledge of the industry. Think of it as the grown-up version of making friends on the playground—only with fewer monkey bars and more business cards.

The Golden 20

Before we start marching out onto the unbeaten path of meeting new people, let's begin our networking with people we already know. Do this by going through the "Golden 20" exercise.

Open up a spreadsheet or get out a piece of paper and divide it into three columns. In the first column list some people you know who you think could be helpful in your job search. Write these out as quickly as possible without thinking too hard.

Here are some questions to spark your memory:

- Who do I know in the industry I'm interested in?
- Who is a generally well-connected and social person?

- Who has been a mentor to me or been invested in my career in the past?
- Who has high status in their field?
- Who does work related to what I am doing/want to do?
- Who works in either the city or the type of company I'd like to work in?

When you have twenty names down in your first column, add a title to the second column: "Helpfulness." Next to each name, give a rating from 0 to 10 as to how likely that person is to assist in your search. If it's your brother-in-law, he's probably a 10 out of 10. If it's someone you met at a conference a few years ago and have stayed in light contact with through social media, they could be a 4. This isn't an exact science; just try to quickly make determinations as to how likely they are to respond to you and give you advice or introductions in your job search.

Finally, title the third column "Influence." Ask yourself: Does that person have any sway in getting you the result you're after? Someone who works at your target company would likely be a 9. Someone who has a modest amount of connections in your general industry may be a 6. This one can be difficult to determine, because you often don't know how connected a person may be. But do your best to make a guess, and if you're deciding between a higher or lower number, go higher.

Now that you have all three columns completed, it should look something like this:

NAME	HELPFULNESS	INFLUENCE
Asher Turner	10	5
Leila Navarro	8	4
Micah Sinclair	5	5
Malik Khan	3	9
Seraphina Blair	3	2

Next, if someone's helpfulness *and* influence scores are each a 4 or below, cross that person off the list for now. We can come back to them later, but right now let's prioritize our time to focus on people who have higher helpfulness and/or influence.

If their *helpfulness* score is an 8 or higher (even if their influence score is low), put it on your to-do list to reach out to that person and tell them what you're looking for in your next career move to see if they know anyone.

If someone's *influence* score is a 6 or above but their *helpfulness* score is 7 or lower, our goal is to increase that person's helpfulness score. You'll do this by building a relationship with that person. Like their posts on LinkedIn, email them saying that you've recommended their speaking event to three of your friends, or utilize one of the other approaches in the 60 Seconds of Value section later in this chapter. Don't ask for anything right away, but do what you can to add value to their lives so that you might be able to request an introduction later. Through that relationship building, their helpfulness score will increase.

Finally, you have the midlevel scores left. These are the people with *helpfulness* scores at or below 7 and *influence* scores at or below 5. Since there is only so much time in a day, you'll focus on these people only after you have had a chance to reach out to or begin deepening the relationship with those mentioned in the previous two paragraphs.

That said, we don't want to write them off quite yet. A person with an influence score of 4 may have an unexpected connection, and another person with a helpfulness score of 6 may surprise you and become your greatest advocate. Therefore, I recommend doing two things. First, add value to them to increase their helpfulness score—so reengage the relationship and find ways to help them or add 60 Seconds of Value. Second, don't wait long to mention you're job searching and ask if they know anyone. We don't want to pour too much time into adding value, the way we might for people with more obviously "influential" connections.

While the quant side of your personality may want to get precise data and follow this formula to perfection, I'll let you know right now, it's not that deep. No sense in debating whether someone is a 5 or a 6 for influence or not reaching out to someone you know you should speak to, just because their score isn't quite right. Instead of getting caught up in the numbers, use this simple exercise as a starting point to take action.

I once had a client who put only two people on her Golden 20 list. Unless your body was cryogenically frozen and now you have been unfrozen one hundred years later to find that everyone you once knew is dead, your list should definitely be longer than two people. The one exception might be if you have moved to a country where you don't know anyone. If that's the case, you'll want to follow the strategies of meeting new people later in this chapter.

It turned out that my client was putting on the list only people who worked at her top-choice company. This is far too narrow, and the likelihood that you already know people at your target companies is slim. The goal isn't to make your list that specific, but instead to open yourself up to the idea that the people you know, know other people.

When you reach out to people in your network, here is a template of what to say:

> Hi, _____, I was thinking about you the other day and wanted to reconnect! What is new with you since we last spoke? It would be great to catch up.

One of the keys to being authentic in networking and increasing your response rates is to be sure to customize every message. While the above message is a good starting point, push yourself to be less generic. Here is an example:

> Hi Laura, I was thinking about you the other day when I saw that new discovery they made on Mars. What is new with you since we last spoke? I just came back from 3 months in Germany, and we are launching a new app, so things have been hectic, but exciting. It would be great to catch up.

Here you're bringing up something specific to the person, as well as modeling the kind of response you're looking for when it comes to hearing an update about their life. Their response should then be followed by an ask to hop on a fifteen-minute call to chat more.

Once you have a chance to speak with them and hear about what they've been up to, update them on your life; this will naturally lead you to mention you're considering landing a new job. At this point you can ask them for advice or if they know anyone in your chosen industry, profession, or target companies.

If it's a great conversation and you see value in staying in contact with them, do the number one thing that ensures you'll stay in their life: get on their calendar. Propose having quarterly catch-up calls. This puts your networking on autopilot—because you two can easily connect four times a year without the uncomfortable feeling of popping up out of nowhere to ask for a call.

Take time now to create your Golden 20 list. Don't overthink your outreach, and view it as reconnecting with a friend rather than networking.

60 Seconds of Value

A cornerstone of networking is generosity and caring for others. One thing that is intimidating about this is that we often feel like we have nothing to give other people. Especially if we are more junior in our careers—we can't imagine a senior associate being able to provide value to a vice president. Yet, this is simply not true. There are lots of ways you can add value, which we'll discuss throughout this section.

Additionally, adding value to others feels like a daunting undertaking that is going to eat up a lot of time. However, this isn't true either. You can find ways to help others that take as little as 60 seconds, no matter what level you're at in your career.

Enter: the 60 Seconds of Value strategy to help others and improve your networking.

The concept of 60 Seconds of Value is simple. When you are interacting with someone, make it your mission to think about ways you can make a small difference in their life. It's incredible how a little thoughtfulness can make a big impression.

In order to add value to a person, though, first you need to know what matters to them. The fatal mistake most professionals make is they simply ask the person what they need help with. It sounds counterintuitive, but this is the worst way to uncover what you need to do to provide value.

> *The laziest phrase in networking is "Let me know if there's anything I can help you with!" Don't say this!*

We say this to people with pure intentions—we truly want to help them. Yet when you ask this, almost no one comes back with a request for your help.

Why?

They aren't sure what you are offering, what you have access to, or how you can help.

Instead of putting it on the other person to come up with ways you can help, ask them some probing questions in your conversation with them.

> *The secret to adding value is to ask good questions and actively listen.*

Here are questions you should ask every person you catch up with on a networking call (or text conversation):

- "What have been your top focuses at work these days?"
- "What are you excited about lately?"
- "What else do you have coming up outside of work?"

These questions, if you listen closely, will give you exactly what you need to add 60 Seconds of Value. The first question gets to the root of what goals they are currently working toward, and what's keeping them up at night. The second question can go personal or professional, and cuts to something that lights that person up. The third question gives you an opportunity to help that person on more of a personal level, which can sometimes be easier to do, but is still incredibly meaningful.

Work these three questions into your conversations. Then, either in the moment, if you're inspired, or that evening after you've parted, come up with a way to help that person. Think *small*. That's the secret. This does not need to be a grand gesture, nor does it need to be impressive. It simply should be thoughtful.

Here are several ways to add 60 Seconds of Value:

1. Make an introduction.

Making introductions is usually what people think of first when imagining ways to add value. This can be demoralizing, because so many job seekers report that they feel like they have a small professional network, and therefore finding people to make introductions to is challenging. But give it a try if you can! If you notice that they are hiring for their accounting team, perhaps you can introduce them to a recruiter you know who specializes in financial roles. If they say they love to go on cruises, you can put them in touch with your friend who works at a cruise company that may be able to get them a deal. Be actively listening to what they enjoy and are focused on to come up with great ideas for introductions.

2. Extend invites to communities.

An absolute necessity for your career is that you should be in communities related to your profession. These could be as simple as online groups and chat groups that you join with a single click. You could also take it a step further and join an official professional society, with meetings, dues, and in-person events. Instead of being a lurker in those groups, who throws a "like" on a post now and then, be an active participant. Comment, engage, and if you're up for it, post. Your presence should be known in the group. Once you join several groups related to your profession and industry, it's a wonderful way to add value to others by inviting them to join as well. For example, I was part of a free online Women in Blockchain group when I worked in that industry. I met a lawyer who commented about the lack of women in the industry, and I gave a quick plug about this online group I was in, how it was a great place to connect with other women, and she could even get clients that way. She enthusiastically took me up on my offer to add her to the group, and what did it take me? All of 60 seconds.

3. Engage on social media.

A very simple way to add 60 Seconds of Value into some-one's life is to engage on social media. If they are active on social media in a professional manner, this makes it especially easy. When they post about a job opening at their company—any job opening—leave a comment saying, "Commenting so that my network can see this great employment opportunity." They will notice and be grateful. Really, when they post anything on social media, take time to leave a comment. Anyone who has posted on social media knows that it's unfortunate to put effort into a post only for no one to respond to it. If the company is launching a product, hosting an event, or having a hiring push, write a social post encouraging your network to check the company out. Then, send the person you're helping an email to let them know you shared the product launch on your socials. I don't care if you have three followers, the simple act of doing this will mean the world to the person you're corresponding with. Additionally, you can write a nice review for the company, draft a recommendation for the professional on LinkedIn, or endorse the person for skills on LinkedIn. Again, this is not about making grand gestures, but instead, taking simple thoughtful actions that they didn't ask you to do.

4. Share resources.

When you've heard a bit about what a person is focused on professionally or doing in their personal life, you can come up with ideas for simple resources you can pass along to them.

If they are evaluating which project management software to use, you may have done a pros and cons list for the different tools, so you can send that along to them. If they say that they are going to Disneyland with their family, you may send an article with tips on how to reduce the wait time for rides. If they are looking to hire a nanny, you can recommend an email list they can join to hear about nannies who are open to work. If they just moved to a new city, you can text a friend who lives there to get recommendations for happy hours or things to do, and then pass that information along to your networking contact. There are so many little ways that you can be helpful; it's a matter of listening to the person and then getting a bit creative with how you can serve them.

5. Brainstorm ideas.

During a networking call, I once had a man say he loved my content so much, and then he sent me a list of topic ideas he had for future videos I could do. It didn't matter so much if the topic list was good, it was more that he took the time to create the list that warmed my heart. So when you are looking to add value into someone's life, how can you come up with ideas that could be helpful? Brainstorming can turn up wide-ranging possibilities; examples include proposing group costume ideas for their upcoming office holiday costume contest, suggesting content creators that the professional could follow that could inspire content creation for the business they work for, and recommending locations where they could affordably host their upcoming conference. Do be wary here, though:

your ideas could come off as patronizing, especially if you try to give strategic advice when you have little context about the business. Every now and then, someone will give me advice for my business that sounds something like, "Here's a tip, a business like yours could benefit from starting a podcast." Yes, thank you, I am aware of the existence of podcasts. These types of comments are a bit unhelpful, because they attempt to be strategic without a full understanding of the business. Stick more with ideas pertaining to already existing initiatives, versus attempting to propose new ones.

So promise me that you'll stop saying, "Let me know if I can help you," unless you *don't* want to help the person. Instead, take it a step further, be thoughtful, and add 60 Seconds of Value. This is how deep relationships are built. Never expect anything in return, and you'll be surprised by the generosity that comes back in your direction over time.

How to Meet New People

Everything you learned as a kid about not talking to strangers gets thrown out the window when we go Job Shopping. You must adopt the mentality that strangers are simply friends you haven't met yet. I've been told by clients that my Job Shopping strategies are an "introvert's dream" because I teach targeted networking approaches—where I don't expect you to walk into a conference and "work the room," but instead focus on meaningful one-on-one interactions. Rather than searching in a venue for the right person to speak to, only to burn a lot of time and energy on polite conversations that are unproductive, we are going to take a more targeted approach to meeting new people. We will walk through how to identify which new people to speak with and how to approach them.

Finding the Right People

When it comes to looking for people to meet who may help them in the job search, I sometimes see my clients make the mistake of being a bit too targeted with their outreach. Often, they will try to network only with people who have the same job title as them, or they will reach out only to hiring managers, or only to influential people in the company with higher titles than them. While it makes sense to prioritize connecting with these types of contacts, this approach is far too narrow. Our goal is to meet people who could ultimately refer you to a job at their company; therefore, being employed at that company is really the only criterion.

Start by picking a target company and sifting through its employees. The best approach is to find someone with something in common with you. You can use search fields to be specific on websites like LinkedIn, where you can narrow down by current company, previous companies (did they work somewhere you've worked?), and alma mater (did you go to the same university?), and you can even search keywords. For example, you might want to find someone who, like you, has volunteered for the Make-A-Wish Foundation. You can type in that organization as a keyword to see if someone at your target company has that on their profile.

Other simple things you can connect with someone on

include being a stay-at-home parent, living in the same city or country at some point, transitioning in your career (such as if you both were formerly teachers), and so on. And of course, a simple thing to have in common is a mutual acquaintance. If that's the case, ask that person to make an introduction, or introduce yourself by first stating that you both know the same person.

Sometimes you simply will find no common ground with anyone at the company. When in doubt, pick someone and reach out anyway. The most important piece is that ideally you don't come across as too generic, so no matter who you contact, be sure that they don't feel like they are receiving a mass email. Let's dive into how to best reach out to the people you've identified at your target companies.

The Approach

In today's job market, it's not about knowing people; it's about *noticing* people. You can easily find the current employees of a company with a simple online search and find a connection point: you can *notice* something about them.

You may say,

> Hi there, I saw that you're a military veteran, just like me, and you made the transition into the technology industry. Would you be open to sharing your story of how you did it? I'm looking to make a similar potential transition.

You're not selling yourself for an open role or talking about what makes you so interesting. Instead, you take an interest in them. You'd be surprised how many people are willing to go to bat for you after you've taken time to form a genuine connection. Too often job seekers focus their outreach messages on their own careers, but this rarely works. People want to feel like they haven't received a mass email and that you are legitimately interested in learning about them.

I recommend reaching out to people via email since most of us tend to check our emails multiple times a day. There are many tools out there to find people's emails; find an up-to-date list at reversethesearch.com/resources.

For each of your target companies, identify three people to reach out to. Start with the person who you think is most likely to respond and reach out to them first. Wait two business days. If they haven't responded yet, follow up with them and send out your first correspondence to the second person on your list for that company. Then two business days later send your second follow-up to the first contact, your first follow-up to the second contact, and your first correspondence to the third contact. If you get a response from any of them, stop the process for that one company and focus your energy toward building the relationship with the contact who responded (while you continue the same process for your other target companies).

Advocates versus Avoiders

During this process, we have to face the fact that some people simply won't interact with you or help you, and that's okay.

> *One of your goals when networking is to identify who is an **Advocate** and who is an **Avoider**.*

An Advocate is someone who responds to your messages, takes time to answer your questions, and genuinely expresses interest in helping you. An Avoider is someone who is slow to respond, challenging to schedule time with, and hesitant to offer additional support. Being honest with ourselves about who is who can help us save time and heartache. We see the signs of an Avoider after a few follow-ups, and let the relationship go. Then when we meet an Advocate, we add value to their lives and keep them in the loop of our progress.

Signs of an Advocate versus an Avoider

ADVOCATE	AVOIDER
Is likely to help enthusiastically, often with no personal gain involved.	May feel obligated to assist due to a preexisting relationship or shared connection.
Responds within three emails (initial, and two follow-ups).	Likely helps begrudgingly or not at all, possibly due to lack of interest or skepticism about networking.
Usually is well-connected and willing to make introductions or offer advice.	May provide limited or unhelpful information, or actively discourage networking efforts.
Tends to be positive and optimistic, offering encouragement and support.	Often requires significant effort and follow-ups to engage.

Digital Proximity

Now, there are other ways to go about networking that are a bit warmer than a cold intro; one way is to increase your digital proximity. It's a lot easier to meet new people if there's an organic connection. For example, you can join professional communities online (they don't have to be official ones with dues—informal chat groups can be wonderful as well), engage with people on social media, and essentially go from an unknown lurker online to someone who is digitally standing next to folks you'd like to meet, ready to strike up a conversation and offer them a piece of gum.

One way this could play out would be that the person you want to meet posts on LinkedIn about an interesting piece of industry news. You then leave a quality comment that explains why you find this post interesting, add your thoughts, and possibly end with a question to the poster. Job seekers often get tripped up here because they think that their comment needs to be incredibly insightful and show off their expertise. Don't put that kind of pressure on yourself! The person who posted will be happy to simply see what you took away from the post, and potentially your personal experience.

> *In all interactions in networking, we need to think less about how we appear to others and instead focus more on making others feel seen.*

After this comment is made you can more seamlessly take the conversation to direct messages, as you are no longer a perfect stranger. It's important to remember that networking is about building relationships, not just collecting contacts.

Take the time to get to know the people you meet and see how you can help each other professionally. Building relationships with the right people in your industry can be an invaluable asset in your career.

Getting Referred

After all of this chatting with new people, the ultimate goal is to get referred to jobs. Being referred means that someone within the company submits your application for you, you submit your application through their personal link associated with the job posting, you apply on the website and your contact alerts the hiring team for you, or they pass along your résumé via email to a person running the hiring process. Essentially all these versions of being referred boil down to one exciting truth: your application is placed in a much shorter pile to be reviewed than all of the online applications.

The first step to getting referred is meeting someone at the target company and having an informational interview, which you now know how to do. Some people will naturally offer to refer you to an open role at their company, but if they don't offer, don't ask on the call. When you hop off the call, shoot them an email along these lines:

Hi [Name],

Thank you so much for chatting with me today about your career and experience at [Company]. Based on everything you shared, I've decided to move forward with applying for the [Job Title] role. I realize that it's common for applications to get lost in the shuffle—any recommendations on how to ensure the application gets seen?

Have a great week!
[Your Name]

Often, people will volunteer to refer you by submitting your application, putting you in touch with the hiring manager, or alerting the recruiter that you are applying. Other times, they will tell you to simply apply online. The good news is that even if you apply online, you can now put in the first sentence of your cover letter that you know this person at the company. What a way to grab the hiring team's attention to show you're not a rando! Then also send an email alerting the hiring manager that you spoke with that contact, and that you are very interested in the company and the role.

When No One Responds and the Clock Is Ticking

You may have thrown this book down as a wave of productivity washed over you and you began your networking process, only to find that despite reaching out to several people at your target company, no one has responded and time is running out.

Now, while I seriously believe that if you are pursuing manager-level and higher roles in your job search, you should make it a rule that you enter company hiring processes *only* through referrals and sourcing, I understand that sometimes you might just be eager to apply, these rules be damned. So here are some sweet tips for you if that is the case. (Side note, if you're going for public sector roles, for sure submit an application. It takes a while, but, unlike the private sector, they actually read all the applications.)

Because you are a Job Shopper, while you may choose to apply online, there's no way that you are going to stop there. We measure our job search in interactions, not applications, remember? So immediately after you apply, you are going to research who you believe the hiring manager to be. This person is usually the one with a title a level above the role you're going for, and depending on the company, their city on their social media profiles can be a clue as to if they are the right person. Too many job seekers are nervous to reach out because they aren't 100 percent sure that they are reaching out to the right person. It's not a big deal if you reach out to the wrong person, though; they can simply forward your message along to the right person.

Your email can sound something like this:

Hi [Name],

Great to meet you! I just applied for the [Job Title] role at [Company], and I wanted to share how interested I am in the position. I [name specific accomplishments that relate to what is listed in the job description]. I am particularly excited by [Company] because [give the reason you like that company].

I took a guess that you are the hiring manager, so if you're not, I'm happy to aim my follow-up emails elsewhere. Otherwise, I look forward to potentially connecting.

Best,
[Name]

I also recommend attaching your résumé to the email and linking your LinkedIn profile. When you send an email like this, know that you're doing the hiring manager a favor. They are exhausted from sifting through poorly crafted résumés and generic job applications. The fact that you popped up in their inbox to show that you truly want this job, and went through the additional effort to show it, makes them hopeful you could be a good fit. Often what happens next is the hiring manager will peek at your application in the system. Ta-da! You have now jumped to the top of the pile.

I was chatting with a group of recruiters who agreed that this strategy of emailing the hiring manager or recruiter has become more common over time. So I asked them, "Is it even worth doing, then?" They gave a resounding "Yes!" You're still in the less than 5 percent of people who do this, and the effort in itself gets the overwhelmed hiring team to take a look.

Now, there is no guarantee that you'll get an interview from this email, and there are many reasons for this. First, the hiring manager possibly didn't read your email. If you are applying for a highly coveted position at a popular brand-name company, this strategy isn't as potent. I'm sure someone who works at a top sports employer and receives an email expressing interest in working there thinks, "You want to work here? So do millions of others." Whereas the hiring manager at the less known Software as a Service company that sells software to help track inventory in retail stores is likely going to be tickled when they see a thoughtful email detailing why a candidate is specifically interested in working at that business.

Second, you may have simply missed the timing. Companies leave roles up on job boards usually until they have a candidate sign the offer letter, or sometimes all the way up until that person's start date. That means that while the role could appear open, the team could be so far into the hiring process, and already have several candidates they are jazzed about, that they aren't going to entertain your application.

Third, they looked at your application and weren't interested. It wasn't strong enough. It wasn't what they were looking for. Simple as that.

As a Job Shopper, networking will be your secret weapon. If you've ever wondered how people can job search without deep bags under their eyes and the inexplicable desire to stare directly into the sun, it's because their network is doing a lot of the hard work for them. We've delved into the nitty-gritty of why it's crucial to have a strong network, and that it's not just about submitting heaps of applications and hoping for the best. Remember, quality over quantity is key. It's all about those meaningful interactions, not just the number of job board submissions.

With the tools and strategies we've explored, you're well equipped to forge connections, add value, and make your Job Shopping a bit, dare I say, fun? Okay, maybe not front-row-seats-at-the-concert fun, but I really hope you enjoy building these relationships, as that is one of the greatest gifts of a job search. When I was laid off from a job, along with 50 percent of the company, the chief product officer, who had unfortunately lost his job as well, looked at me reassuringly and said, "Our networks are about to blossom." And that's what I know will be true for you, too, as you start your Job Shopping journey.

Key Takeaways

- Shift your focus to interactions, not applications. And if you do submit an application, be sure to follow it up by getting in contact with someone at the company.

- Start with familiar connections by utilizing the Golden 20 exercise. Identify potential allies in your network who could aid in your job search, and prioritize outreach based on their perceived helpfulness and influence.

- Implement the 60 Seconds of Value strategy. Use probing questions to understand your networking contacts' needs and interests, and then add value to their lives in small ways.

- Reach out to people you don't know by crafting authentic and customized outreach messages. Approach conversations with genuineness and curiosity, focusing on learning about the other person rather than solely seeking job opportunities.

- Implement a systematic follow-up process with initial contacts, alternating between multiple individuals if necessary. Prioritize individuals who actively engage and offer support (Advocates) over those who are unresponsive or hesitant (Avoiders).

- Engage with professional communities online and use social media to increase digital proximity and build warmer connections.

- Conduct informational interviews to potentially secure referrals for job applications.

- Email the hiring manager or recruiter after applying for a position to express interest and potentially gain attention amidst the application pool.

- Remain persistent in networking efforts, adapting strategies based on responses and industry norms, while accepting that not all interactions will yield immediate results.

Chapter 7

GET ON THE SAME SIDE OF THE INTERVIEW TABLE

A fter months of working on becoming a Job Shopper, Lisa found herself in a formal interview for a government job. If you've experienced an interview for a government job before, you know it's structured. Each interview follows a specific set of questions, not drifting away from the core script.

The interview was ending and Lisa asked, "Do you happen to have a few extra minutes for questions?" That was the moment everything changed.

They said, "Absolutely," and Lisa began directing the conversation by both asking questions and highlighting things that didn't come up in the interview. She asked about dynamics of the different roles on the team, the projects the department had been working on, and key outcomes for the role at hand. Lisa then responded to the interviewer's answers with "I noticed X and Y about your project. Have you ever thought of doing Z to improve the results?" The hiring manager stopped and stared at Lisa before saying, "See, that right there is what we've been missing, someone who has the expertise not to just do the core job, but to really improve the project and move it forward."

What Lisa did that ultimately landed her the job was that she didn't let the interview pass her by without ensuring the interviewer got to truly see why she would be the best fit for the role.

Job seekers often see the job interview as something that needs to be completely driven by the interviewer. The issue with this is that it relies on the interviewer to extract all of the important information from you, and if they don't ask the right questions, they won't get to know certain important details about your experience that would influence their decision. Additionally, this often leads to the assumption that, especially in structured interviews, you as the candidate can't ask questions, request more time, or share information outside of what has been asked of you. Quite to the contrary, hiring managers appreciate this help, and your initiative leaves an incredible impression.

> *When someone interviews you, their hope is that you will be the perfect candidate.*

Don't regard the interviewer as your adversary or as the one fully controlling the exchange. Instead, be an active participant who guides the narrative.

Once you view yourself as an equal to the interviewer, you will then have two missions during the encounter:

1. Build rapport with the interviewer, just like you would with a coworker.
2. Use what I call the "Consultative Approach," and imagine that you are a consultant who must figure out the company's biggest pain points and how you would solve them.

Finally, I'll send you on a secret side mission: build a 90-Day Plan while you're in the interview process. Whether you end up unveiling the 90-Day Plan to the hiring team or not, this exercise will allow you to get in the Consultative mindset and ask the right questions in the interview process.

These are collaborative approaches to ensure that you're the right person for the job. Let's walk through each of these elements to get you mentally on the same side of the interview table as your interviewer.

Passing the Likability Test

There is a secret test that every single hiring manager will put you through. It's the "Do I like them?" test, and it's one that we often forget to prepare for. Working in human resources, I clearly saw how interviewers often decide whether or not they like you, and then back up their subjective conclusions with a rationalization.

Most hiring managers can't help but consider the personality that comes along with the skill set. Oftentimes, a hiring manager will choose someone who is easier to communicate with, friendly, and appears enthusiastic about the role, over someone who is more qualified but lacks those traits.

In order to pass the likability test, you'll need to work on three key components: voice and energy, building rapport, and aiming for a mutual fit. Let's walk through each so that you are establishing excellent relationships with your interviewers.

Voice and Energy

I once had a client, Wilson, who was a sales executive. He had interviews at seven companies lined up, which led to three final-round interviews . . . and zero offers. Looking at his résumé, he was clearly an impressive candidate, and talking to him was an absolute pleasure. I was confused as to why anyone would pass on him. In order to help him, I started asking mock interview questions, and something about him changed.

As soon as we stepped into "mock interview mode," his voice sounded stilted and singsongy. He didn't sound like Wilson. I stopped him and said, "Wilson, I am pausing the mock interview right now. I have a quick question for you: You mentioned on your résumé that you revamped the processes for the overseas team. What did that entail?" Wilson relaxed and dove into what he meant and described a great accomplishment that had major ripple effects throughout the sales organization.

When he finished, I said, "Wilson, I lied. I didn't pause the mock interview. That's the question I would have asked as the interviewer, but I wanted you to lose your Interview Voice and instead talk to me like a real person. Your answer was incredible and so natural!"

The truth is, your voice shouldn't change based on if you are in an interview or not. At least, not in the way so many of us do. Too many of us do an "Interview Voice" that we think makes us seem professional, but really we come across as fake. People don't want to work with an unsettlingly polite robot, they want to work with a dynamic, interesting person. Use your natural voice.

Another issue I commonly see is someone bringing very little energy to the interview. Appearing on a video interview may add ten pounds, but it also subtracts three cups of coffee, so you have to bring more energy than you normally would in a typical meeting or conversation.

One of my clients was monotone in the way he answered things in his mock interview. I told him to redo one of his answers but have his enthusiasm be completely over the top. "You should feel silly," I told him. He redid his answer and he looked . . . normal. Honestly, he was even still a bit underenergized.

Here is an exercise I recommend you do if you think you may have calm energy that could be interpreted as low energy. Record yourself answering an interview question in a way that feels over the top. Watch it back, and ideally have someone else watch it, too. What do you sound like? How do you feel watching this more energized version of yourself? Odds are, as long as you aren't doing a fake Interview Voice along with it, that you just dramatically increased your likability in the interview by upping the energy, which translates to enthusiasm and confidence.

To review, check for these issues:

	THE ISSUE	THE FIX
INTERVIEW VOICE	You use a robotic or singsongy tone as your "professional" voice.	Practice answering interview questions as if a friend or coworker asked.
LACK OF ENERGY	You may be a naturally lower energy person, but that comes across on video as aloof and uninterested.	Record yourself doing a highly energetic interview and then have someone review it and tell you how you come across. Often you will appear normal (or still not energetic enough!).

Most people need to work on one or more of these three things when it comes to interviewing, so be sure to record yourself over time, checking for these elements.

Build Rapport

Next, it's time to befriend the interviewer. While this may not immediately sound professional, imagine for a second that you already have the job. How would you act around this person? You would be friendly, ask them about their day, and take a personal interest in them. You wouldn't sit there, anxiously waiting for them to grant you permission to speak. In other words, **treat small talk like a big deal.**

A simple way to do this is to practice your answers to the "throwaway" questions—these usually sound something like:

- "How was your weekend?"
- "How is your day going?"
- "Where are you located?"

> On the surface, it seems like these questions are asked before the interview starts, but these may be some of the most important questions you get in an interview.
>
> That is because the way you answer these questions determines your first impression—an interpretation of you that, once solidified, is difficult to change.

So instead of responding simply with "Good" when asked how your day is going, say something with a bit more personality. It could sound like, "My day is going great, I've nearly finished drinking my entire water jug. It doesn't sound like much, but I always feel better when I do."

Okay, that statement was incredibly mundane. But that's the point. You don't need to say something brilliant, you just need to say *something*. So much of small talk is simply volunteering insignificant pieces of information to move the conversation forward. By saying things like this, you come across as more friendly and in control. You're helping to move the conversation along, and you may even connect with the interviewer as he pulls out his water bottle, covered in stickers, that he cherishes and carries with him everywhere like a lap dog.

Aim for a Mutual Fit

One fatal mistake job seekers make when trying to be likable in the interview is agreeing to everything. I once brought two candidates into an interview, let's call them Dan and Chloe. They were similarly qualified, yet in every interview, Chloe was hands-down the favorite choice.

I had to find out why.

After Chloe's interviews, interviewers said, "She's sharp, we need her."

After Dan's interviews, they said, "I'm not sure . . ."

As I studied the interview feedback and spoke with the hiring panel in the debrief, it was clear. What appealed to the hiring panel was that Chloe knew herself and had a perspective. In her interview, Chloe did not shy away from detailing the kind of opportunity she wanted versus what she did not want. She laid it out very clearly and asked probing questions to make sure it was a mutual fit. She was direct about her strengths, and clear with both the areas she didn't have experience in but was excited to grow, and the areas she was uninterested in exploring.

Meanwhile, Dan was affirmative on everything and simply agreed with what the interviewers said. He showed no preference for different tasks on the job, saying he liked all of it and felt confident in all of his skills for it. His highly positive attitude and openness to say, "I'll do whatever you need!" left the interviewers feeling unsure, like they didn't get to know Dan on a deeper level.

It's like offering to grab someone a drink at a bar. If you

ask, "What do you want?" and they say, "Whatever, I like anything!" you're probably going to be a bit frustrated. This person may feel like they are being easy, but really, you want to make sure you get them something they will enjoy, and their complete lack of a preference makes you lose a bit of confidence that they will like the drink you choose. Any sort of a preference, even as simple as "If they have a specialty cocktail with tequila, that's my choice! Otherwise I'll have the house red," would be preferred.

Job Shoppers always come to the interview with a perspective on exactly what they want in their next role, and companies absolutely love it. It shows that the Job Shopper is looking for a mutual fit, and it gives the company an opportunity to rise to those standards. When a Job Shopper states what they are looking for in their next opportunity and it matches what the company can offer, that solidifies the hiring panel's confidence that this candidate would be a great hire.

A candidate who is looking for a mutual fit is more likely to understand the company's goals and values and will be able to align their own goals and experiences with those of the company. This can lead to a more productive and engaged employee who is more likely to be committed to the company's mission and stay with the company for an extended period of time. Moreover, a good mutual fit means that the candidate is more likely to be satisfied with their job, which leads to less turnover and recruitment cost for the company.

By asking great questions, listening actively, and conducting research, you can be almost certain that your perspective on what you want for the role aligns with what the company is looking for.

For example, I was once being interviewed for a head of human resources role at a growing technology company. From talking to the hiring manager and reading the job description, it was clear that they weren't looking for a human resources professional who was there for a purely administrative role. They were looking for someone with more of a strategic mind. So when they asked what I wanted in my next role, I did not say, "This role all sounds great, I like all of it and know I could be good at it." I instead said,

> "As I am considering moving jobs to my next opportunity, the role has to be at a company that values human resources as a strategic function. I am good at the administrative side of HR, but if that is more than 50 percent of my time in the role, it's not the right opportunity for me."

Immediately the hiring manager jumped in and started selling me on this role. He assured me that the role would be strategic, reiterated how much he values the HR function, and even went on to describe why he saw me as a great fit for the role, completely unprompted.

So, take what you learned in earlier chapters along your Job Shopping journey and be sure to know yourself, know what you want, do your research, and be clear to the interviewer that you are looking for a mutual fit. That is absolutely irresistible to a hiring manager. They feel so confident in giving you the offer because they know it's exactly what you want, and they believe you'll stay at the business long term.

A final note on connecting with your interviewer: remember that the interviewer is actually rooting for you. They aren't doing all these interviews for kicks because they don't have any other work to do. Quite the opposite: they can't wait to find the right candidate so that they can stop interviewing and get back to their main job. That means they are hopeful when they get in an interview with you that you will be the one who makes them say, "We found the person! We can stop looking, this is the one!"

Come into the interview with that perspective. You both want the same thing. This is not an adversarial dynamic where they are there to try to tear you down, and you're out here trying to survive. Instead, they invited you to this interview for a reason. Prove them right.

The Consultative Approach

What would it look like to approach a job interview as if you were a consultant to the company, here to create a plan to help them?

You would likely approach it with a mindset of understanding the client's (i.e., the company's) needs and goals, getting a sense of how you can add value, and then proposing a plan to address those needs. The ultimate Job Shopper move is to go into the interview with a Consultative Approach, so for every interview from now on, I want you to go into your conversations with this mentality:

> *"I am the consultant; what information do I need to address the client's needs?"*

Your first step is to do your research on "the client." That includes reviewing the company website, reading their blog, looking them up in the news, and scrolling through their social media. Then, be sure you understand the broader context of the industry, such as identifying their competitors, and listening to podcasts and interviews to hear expert perspectives.

Do everything in your power to experience the company, especially in ways that would directly impact your role. Take yourself through the customer journey to see what it would be like to buy their product or service. If you're going for a marketing role, you better be on their email list. If you're going for a user experience designer role, come to your interview ready to share your experience clicking their links and navigating the pages of their website. If you're pursuing a product role, do what you can to experience their product, such as downloading their app—even if just a free trial—and spend time as a user. If you're in human resources, you can read reviews online of what it's like to work at the company, or interpret culture-related messaging on their socials and blog. You can't be expected to come into the interview fully knowing about everything for the role, but you can get creative to get to know the business.

The second piece is to bring notes to your interview. A consultant wouldn't walk into a meeting empty-handed without their prework, just as you wouldn't go into a major meeting without your documents or presentation. Job seekers often feel weird about bringing notes into an interview, as if that's "cheating" to reference them. But if you view the interview this way, you are not thinking like a Job Shopper. You are thinking an interview is where the company is testing you, and it is your role to pass. While some job interviews are literally that (they are exams or skills tests), most of them are not.

When you are referencing your notes, it's not to read your script for "What's your greatest weakness?" nor are your notes answers to skills questions such as "What is a vlookup?" No, these notes are your research about the business, insights you gained from your other interviews, and questions you hope to ask the interviewer. Put another way: it's simply the notes you would bring into a meeting as a hired consultant.

When planning the questions to ask in the interview, think like a consultant trying to get the information necessary to do their job, not like a person hoping to impress the interviewer (though ironically, the former is actually what impresses them). I hear many job seekers spending their time asking the most common question to interviewers, "What's your favorite part about working here?" This question in itself is not bad, and the positive is that it gets the interviewer talking about themselves, but it is purely rapport building and doesn't create a rich discussion. I provide a list of questions to ask in an interview in the supplemental document at reversethesearch.com/resources, but know that you're on the right track if each of your questions is unique to the particular opportunity. Your questions should be based on either your research about the company or things you've learned in the interview process.

Write these questions down ahead of your interview so that you already have a clear idea of what you would like to ask, and then write additional questions down as they come to mind during your interview. Most companies are not only okay with you asking questions, but they heavily prefer candidates who do.

> *I have run thousands of interview debrief sessions, and interviewers would consistently remark on how great the candidates' questions were—not answers, questions!*

That is because questions can show deep understanding, curiosity, and intellect. It can also show engagement in a way that makes the employer more confident that the candidate is vetting the opportunity as well, and therefore feels like a great mutual-fit discussion. Most interviewers aren't on some sick power trip (though some definitely are), and actually much prefer a lively conversation about the work.

Here is an example of a question I might ask in an interview for a human resources role, based on my research as a "consultant":

- "With the organization doubling in size since last year, how has that impacted the organizational culture?"

I would ask this to understand what areas of the business may need special attention and intervention from human resources. The interviewer might say that people are lacking training, company processes aren't scaling, or communication lines are unclear. As a consultant, I am taking note of the areas where I could potentially be most impactful.

Here is a question I may ask based on previous interviews in the process:

- "Holly mentioned in my interview with her that she saw the most important need right now from the human resources department as streamlining the hiring process. Is that your view as well? What else would you hope this role would focus on?"

I would ask this question to get clear on priorities. Each department will likely have a different perspective on what would be the most valuable focus of your role, so it's good to ask multiple people to get a full picture.

Next is the importance of follow-up questions. Having a good baseline of preset questions is helpful, but where you'll get the most helpful information is through quality follow-ups. For example, if you were to ask the previous question about streamlining the hiring process, and the interviewer agreed that it is a priority, you may ask:

- "What is the current hiring process?"
- "What do you see as the areas for improvement?"
- "What do you think is the easiest change that could be made to the hiring process that would make a big difference?"

No matter what their answer is for priorities, you better be digging in further. Because remember, you're imagining that you are a consultant who has to scurry off to solve these challenges after these conversations, so you need to get the full story.

Ultimately, through your incisive questions, you should be piecing together a 90-Day Plan while you interview. This is an incredibly impactful strategy that will impress your interviewer with your ability to go above and beyond.

The 90-Day Plan

The final step toward being an active participant in your interview is developing a 90-Day Plan that you will carry out in the role once you get the offer.

A 90-Day Plan is a strategic outline or road map that details your goals, priorities, and action steps for the first 90 days in a new job or role. The reasons you should create one are numerous:

1. The simple act of zeroing in on what you'll need to do in the first 90 days will lead you to do more focused research and ask better questions in your interviews.
2. You can bring the 90-Day Plan into your later-round interviews (typically third round or later) and impress your interviewer by how thoughtful you are about understanding the role.
3. You get to engage in a deeper conversation about the role, giving you greater insight on whether or not this is the right fit for you.
4. The interviewer will be picturing you clearly in the role, further solidifying your odds of landing the offer.

The plan does not have to be super detailed, but it should contain overarching goals, key deliverables for those goals, and a rough timeline of when those deliverables will be met, either by week or by month.

A misconception is that the plan needs to be correct. Not so. Rather, it is more of a powerful tool to help you ask the right questions as you continue your interviews and to guide you in productive discussion.

Here are the steps to create a 90-Day Plan:

- **Research:** Study the job description and aspects of the business and industry that are relevant to the role you're interviewing for. This could be reading news articles, exploring the company's website, using its product, reading reviews, listening to earnings calls, and so on.
- **Inquire:** In true Consultative Approach fashion, ask questions in your interviews to deeply understand the current state of the business, how this role fits with the team, and what this job is expected to accomplish.
- **Draft:** Write up a rough outline of what you'd imagine the first 90 days would look like.
- **Share:** If there is the right moment, share your 90-Day Plan, ideally in the interview or in an email between interviews with the hiring manager.

Creating a 90-Day Plan is essentially an exercise in problem-solving. You're identifying problems or goals and proposing solutions. This approach translates seamlessly into your question-asking strategy. When you pose questions, you're essentially asking about the company's pain points and opportunities for improvement. This shows that you're not just interested in the job; you're genuinely focused on helping the company succeed.

As you're asking these questions, you're not saying that it's for a 90-Day Plan; that is the secret side mission that only you know, until the time is right to share.

Continuing our example of a human resources director asking questions to create their 90-Day Plan, after several interviews where they learn that the hiring process needs to be streamlined, they may come up with this:

90-Day Plan—Human Resources Director

Month 1: Assess and Understand
- *Weeks 1–2:* Meet with department heads and key stakeholders to understand their hiring needs and challenges.
- *Weeks 3–4:* Review current hiring processes and identify bottlenecks or inefficiencies.

Month 2: Strategic Planning and Team Alignment
- *Weeks 5–6:* Develop a strategic plan to streamline the hiring process, focusing on reducing time-to-hire and improving candidate experience.
- *Weeks 7–8:* Communicate the plan to HR team members and allocate resources as needed.

Month 3: Implementation and Monitoring
- *Weeks 9–10:* Implement changes to the hiring process, eliminating identified bottlenecks.

- **Weeks 11–12:** Start tracking KPIs like time-to-fill, cost-per-hire, and candidate satisfaction. Make necessary adjustments based on performance data and feedback.

This plan isn't groundbreaking. It isn't complex. Nonetheless, it gets you in the right headspace to be a Job Shopper and is going to get your hiring manager energized in the conversation. I guarantee that you will be the only candidate who has created a 90-Day Plan.

Now the moment we've all been waiting for—sharing your 90-Day Plan. Imagine this: you walk into the interview armed with a comprehensive plan for your first 90 days on the job. It's like showing up to a potluck dinner with a home-made lasagna while everyone else brought store-bought chips. You're already a standout!

You'll want this to happen in a later interview with the hiring manager, such as a third-round interview or later. People tend to overthink it, but it's actually pretty simple to work your 90-Day Plan into the conversation. Here are several examples; you'll only need one!

Tell me about your leadership style.

My leadership style is collaborative and results-oriented, and I tend to adapt my leadership to the person I'm interacting with. I have been envisioning how I would lead the team at your company and took some time last night to put together a first draft of a 90-Day Plan. Would you be interested in seeing it?

What interests you in this role?

What stood out to me about this role is X, Y, and Z. I've been so interested in the work that I took time this weekend to jot down a 90-Day Plan for the role, would you like to see it?

Why should we hire you?

I've taken time to understand the role, and I wrote out a first draft of a 90-Day Plan for the role and how I could add value. Should we walk through it?

Let's say you get through the whole interview and there was truly not a place that you could weave in your plan. Don't panic! You can respond to the question, "Any other questions for me?" with, "Yes, I jotted down a draft of a 90-Day Plan for this role. Could I show it to you to see if we share an understanding of what this role would entail?" Or if the interview is over, offer to email the 90-Day Plan to the hiring manager so that they can review it after the call.

If there were anything close to having a magic elixir to make you confident in the interview, crafting a 90-Day Plan would be it. You'll feel so capable asking questions to understand whether the challenges the company faces align with your skills and interests. You can also draw parallels with what you have previously worked on to understand the intricacies of what your potential new role would entail.

There's a shift that happens in the interview when you stop talking about your experience and trying to prove that your skills can do the job, and start discussing how you will achieve things in *this* role. The former is the lot of a job seeker looking to get a job; the latter is that of a Job Shopper who is essentially already being viewed as a coworker.

Go from Job Seeker to Consultative Job Shopper

Now we're ready to shift to the same side of the interview table, just as Lisa did at the beginning of this chapter. She entered the interview as if she were a consultant for the department, equal in stature and autonomy. Her interviewer was relieved to finally have a candidate who felt like a coworker and collaborator, and she was promptly short-listed and then offered the job.

So, here's your action item: Using this chapter as a guide, prepare for each job interview thoroughly. Take time to research the interviewer, practice your small talk, and video-record yourself answering questions to ensure your answers are genuine and confident. Then study the company, take great notes, bring your notes into the interviews, and craft your 90-Day Plan. Embrace these strategies and enter your interviews as a true Job Shopper. Go out there and ace those interviews with authenticity, energy, and a clear vision for success!

Key Takeaways

- Maintain authenticity in your voice, avoid a robotic or singsongy tone, and bring enthusiasm to appear confident and engaging.

- Build rapport by approaching small talk with genuine interest and using throwaway questions such as "How are you?" as opportunities to connect with the interviewer.

- Aim for a mutual fit by being clear about your preferences, strengths, and areas for growth.

- Embrace the Consultative Approach by adopting the mindset of a consultant, thoroughly researching the company, bringing notes to the interview, and asking insightful questions.

- Develop a 90-Day Plan by piecing together insights from the interview to formulate a plan for addressing the company's challenges and showcasing your proactive approach.

Chapter 8

BECOME THE
IRRESISTIBLE CANDIDATE

My client James was going for director of human resources roles and made it to the final-round interview at four different companies, but never got a job offer. He had what I call the "Silver Medal Curse," where companies would say, "We really liked you, but we went with someone else." James continually got the silver medal in the hiring process, when really all that matters is the gold.

This was incredibly frustrating for James, because it obviously wasn't a matter of whether or not he was qualified. It was clear that he had what it took to do these jobs, but he would lose the role by mere centimeters to other candidates, for reasons so subtle that he could never perceive what went wrong.

The strategies you will learn next are the interviewing essentials that completely turned around James's job search luck. After implementing these key approaches, he landed job offers at the next four companies he interviewed with, and ultimately accepted a role that was an $80,000 salary increase above his previous job.

When preparing for a job interview, it's certainly important to practice the top interview questions. You know the ones: Tell me about yourself, Why do you want this job, Why did you leave your last job, and so on. I have created hours of videos online that address those top interview questions, so I recommend you check those out.

But in this chapter we are going to go much deeper than practicing a few predictable answers. These strategies are so advanced that your interviews will elevate to a universe only Job Shoppers occupy. The universe James floats in, where he collects four job offers back-to-back. When job seekers hear this, they think that my clients do wacky and out-of-the-box things to stand out, such as show up to the office and perform a rap on why they should be hired, write a thank-you letter on a giant cake, or send a package to the hiring manager containing only one shoe with the note enclosed, "Just trying to get my foot in the door."

While these things are charming and headline-worthy, they aren't going to land you back-to-back offers. Once you learn the strategies, you'll notice that they are psychologically proven tools to build trust and make the high ticket sale of your expertise.

An okay way to persuade a hiring team to choose you is to describe what it would be like to work with you. A good way is to tell stories about your work. And the best way is to *show* them exactly how you work. In order to make yourself into the best, most irresistible candidate, we are going to focus on practicing and executing the latter two with strategies called Story Toolbox and Show-Don't-Tell.

The Story Toolbox

If there is one thing that will supercharge your interview, it's creating a Story Toolbox. The Story Toolbox is your secret stash of carefully crafted stories of things you accomplished in your past jobs, handpicked to showcase your skills and experiences in the best light. Imagine feeling prepared for nearly every interview question a company throws at you—that's a likely reality if you go all in on creating your Story Toolbox. These stories are your solution to connect with potential employers on a deeper level.

When I was a recruiter doing hundreds of phone interviews, I decided to conduct my own study. For dozens of calls I wrote a tally mark each time a candidate, without being prompted to, gave a specific example instead of talking in generalities or saying what they "usually" do. When I looked at the candidates who made it to third-round interviews or later, they were often giving 30 to 40 percent more specific examples and stories than people who tended to be rejected earlier.

This is because stories are like the evidence in a compelling case for your candidacy. They demonstrate your character traits and provide solid proof of your capabilities. For example, if you were to ask someone, "What kind of leader are you?" they could attempt to describe their leadership style with some adjectives and frameworks. But imagine instead, after giving a brief overview of their leadership philosophy, they then dove into an example of when team morale was low, revenue was down, and they were able to alter their strategy and motivate the team to an incredible turnaround. The latter helps you to picture working with this person much more easily, right?

Additionally, the human mind is hardwired to prefer hearing stories over information. In an experiment led by Chip Heath, a professor at Stanford University, students were asked to deliver one-minute speeches on nonviolent crime. The majority of students opted for a data-centric approach, incorporating an average of 2.5 statistics into their speeches, and only one out of every ten students chose to employ storytelling as their method. When Heath later surveyed the students about their recollection of the speeches, the results were striking. A substantial 63 percent of the audience remembered the stories conveyed during the presentations, while a mere 5 percent could recall a single statistic.[*]

This may go without saying, but a company never hired a candidate who they couldn't remember. It's the memorable candidates (well . . . the good kind of memorable) who are fast-tracked through the process and given top-of-the-range job offers.

Crafting Your Story Toolbox

Your first step is to brainstorm stories that can go in your toolbox. This is truly a memory exercise, so do your best to

---

[*] Chip Heath and Dan Heath, *Made to Stick: Why Some Ideas Survive and Others Die* (New York: Random House, 2007).

come up with examples for each prompt below. Memories tend to fall through the cracks, though, so here are some ideas of ways to help you remember:

- Look through old files, emails, job descriptions, and résumés from job searches past
- Sift through old notebooks
- Call up a former coworker and talk through some of the major initiatives you worked with them on to see if they can help spark a memory
- Review old photos, social posts, and texts that are work related

One thing that works for my clients is to read the prompts, do your best to respond to them, and then come back to them once a day for five minutes, or as inspiration strikes. It's pretty amazing how your brain is masterfully working in the background to remember these stories.

Do note that all of these stories should be from the past ten years (with some rare exceptions, such as if it's your only example of utilizing an important skill set for this job). Companies want to hear what you have been up to lately, not what you dealt with in another lifetime. For example, I asked a client to tell me her greatest accomplishment pertaining to the role she was interested in, and her answer began, "Well, twenty years ago . . ." I stopped her right there. If a company asks for your best accomplishment, and you have to go back twenty years, it gives the impression that you haven't done much since. Prioritize telling stories from the past five years, with some potentially spanning ten years.

Here are seven prompts to help you brainstorm stories. Come up with at least two situations for each prompt. You don't need to explain the story yet, simply jot down the idea using enough words that you can recognize what you are referencing.

A time when you saved the day / solved a big problem:

1. _____

2. _____

A time when you collaborated on a team and were able to help others:

1. _____

2. _____

A time when you took charge and were a leader:

1. _____

2. _____

A time when you worked with a difficult person and how you handled it:

1. _____

2. _____

A time you messed up or failed:

1. _____

2. _____

A time when you overcame a major obstacle:

1. _____

2. _____

A time you achieved something great:

1. _____

2. _____

Here is an example of what one of these prompts might look like:

A time when you overcame a major obstacle:
1. Legal dispute when driver didn't get a background check
2. Technology outage that halted production for several days

Remember, you are simply getting these ideas down on paper in a way that has enough information for you to recall the story.

Once you have completed the seven prompts, give yourself a pat on the back. Why? Because you are now able to answer nearly every behavioral question in an interview, and most other interview questions as well. "How is this possible?" you may be asking yourself. "I only responded to seven prompts!"

Well, the magic here is that the stories you came up with can be generalized to thousands of interview questions. All it takes is a bit of creativity, and some tweaking of how you introduce the story and conclude it.

For example, let's say you came up with the following story for this prompt:

A time when you collaborated on a team and were able to help others:
1. Mentored a junior developer, leading to significant productivity improvements

This was a time where you noticed that a junior developer was struggling to hit deadlines and it was dragging down the team. Instead of complaining to management, taking over the work yourself, or continuing to have deadlines slip, you took it upon yourself to mentor her each morning. You identified the key areas where she was getting stuck, and within two weeks she was performing at full capacity and delivering on time.

The nifty thing is, this answer works well for a near limitless number of questions:

- Give an example of when you did something in your role without being asked.
- Tell me about a time when you missed a deadline, and what you did about it.
- Tell me about a time when you worked with an underperformer—how did you handle it?
- What is your leadership style?
- Describe a challenge you faced in the workplace and how you overcame it.
- What would make you a good manager?

Notice most of these are behavioral interview questions (as indicated by asking for examples), but some of them are not, such as "What is your leadership style?" and "What would make you a good manager?" The brilliance of the Story Toolbox is that you can use it for questions that don't even ask for examples.

When asked "What would make you a good manager?" most people would simply describe what would make them a good manager, like this:

I believe I would make a good manager because I have been repeatedly recognized by my managers for effective communication and taking the lead in their absence, and I voluntarily take on mentorship duties without being asked. These qualities reflect my ability to foster a collaborative and productive work environment while ensuring that tasks are accomplished efficiently and team members are supported in their growth and development.

Additionally, my commitment to clear and open communication helps build trust and transparency within the team, facilitating effective problem-solving and decision-making processes. My proactive approach to mentorship not only aids in team members' professional development but also contributes to overall team cohesion and success. In sum, these attributes collectively demonstrate my potential to excel as a manager who leads by example and prioritizes both team and organizational success.

Okay, that's a fine answer. But this answer currently has a lot of self-describing, and frankly, it's not terribly convincing or memorable. What would be better is if, instead of focusing on describing why you think you'd make a good manager, you *show* the interviewer by explaining a situation that illustrates your character. You want every interview answer to say something deeper about what it would be like to work with you, and how you approach work.

Instead of the answer above, use a story from your toolbox and respond like this:

I believe I would make a good manager because I have been repeatedly recognized by my managers for effective communication and taking the lead in their absence, and I voluntarily take on mentorship duties without being asked. For example, in my most recent role I noticed a junior developer was struggling to meet deadlines, which was affecting the entire team's performance.

In this situation, instead of resorting to complaining to management or taking over the work myself, I took a proactive approach. I recognized the importance of mentoring and guiding my team members to help them grow and improve. I approached the junior developer and offered to mentor her each morning before work started. She appreciated the support and accepted my offer.

During our mentoring sessions, I carefully assessed her challenges and identified the specific areas where she was encountering difficulties. We worked together to address those challenges, focusing on improving her time management, problem-solving skills, and coding techniques. I provided constructive feedback and guidance to help her overcome her obstacles.

Over the course of two weeks, thanks to our dedicated morning mentoring sessions, the junior developer showed remarkable improvement. She started delivering her work on time and began to contribute positively to the team's overall productivity. This experience not only helped her professional growth but also demonstrated my ability as a manager to lead by example, communicate effectively, and empower team members to achieve their full potential.

The power of this answer is it helps the interviewer to imagine you in the role. Notice how the story from the toolbox is adapted to be the perfect answer by the introduction of the answer setting the stage, and the final sentence bringing the story back to the topic.

Reflect on each of the fourteen stories you brainstormed earlier. What different kinds of questions can you think of where that story could be an answer?

Draft Your Answers with the CAR Method

Now it's time to flesh out your ideas into full-on "we need to hire this person" stories. We will craft these stories with behavioral interview questions in mind, though as mentioned before, you can use these stories for all kinds of questions. Behavioral interview questions, which ask candidates to provide specific examples of how they have handled certain situations in the past as a predictor of their future performance on the job, are becoming increasingly common in job interviews.

The most common way to answer behavioral questions is to use the STAR Method. STAR stands for Situation, Task, Action, Result. Unpopular opinion, but I believe the four-step process of the STAR Method is one step too long. You don't have to be a graduate from The Juilliard School to know that when telling a story there are most commonly three acts: a beginning, middle, and end. So I teach the three-step CAR Method because it has the appropriate number of steps; CAR stands for:

- **Challenge:** Give context as to the challenge you were up against in the situation. People often give too many details here, but really all the interviewer needs to understand is what you were working on and any major dynamics at play.
- **Action:** Describe the actions you took to tackle the situation. Get specific about what you did, the decisions you made, and the skills you brought to the table. Highlight your role and contributions.
- **Result:** Finish strong by sharing the outcome of your actions. Did you achieve your goal? What happened as a direct result of your efforts? If you can, throw in some numbers or percentages to quantify your success. If you can't quantify, that's okay; did anyone make any positive comments about your performance?

Now it's time to use the CAR Method to scope out each of the stories that you jotted down in your Story Toolbox.

Do your best to think back on those situations and sketch out the Challenge, Action, and Result of each.

Being precise with details can be tough the farther out you are from when that event happened. If you truly can't remember much of the details, it would be best to remove the story from your toolbox or rank the story as a "last resort" example. But you may be surprised at how you're able to remember some of the bigger moments of a project when you put your mind to it. If the interviewer gets very detailed with you, such as asking, "When you submitted the report, how many hours did it take for the person to respond with their edits?" You can give an estimate, "I believe it was the same day." Or if it's way too specific and too long ago to remember, you could say something like, "Unfortunately my memory is failing me since that was six years ago, but I don't recall them ever taking too long."

Take time to actually write down each of your stories. This will take a while, but will be so worth it! Keep in mind: you're not writing a script, so you can write these stories in bullet point format. While it's important to know what you're going to say before you get into the interview, you should never be memorizing, or worse, reading your answers in an interview.

Prioritize the Stories

The next step is to rank your stories and prioritize the best ones. You'll want to narrow them down to your top three stories. This is to make it as easy as possible for you to zero in on your greatest hits before digging into the bottom of the barrel of second-tier stories during an interview.

The best way to choose your top three stories, the ones that you'll focus on telling in most interviews, is to make sure they meet the following criteria:

1. **Highly relevant to the role you're interviewing for.** I know you may have some really cool accomplishments from your past that showcase some interesting transferable skills, but if it's not immediately obvious how this story relates to the role you're going for, it probably shouldn't be in your top three.

2. **Impressive.** An impressive accomplishment can take several forms. It can be impressive because you achieved something great, of course. But it can also be impressive because it shows your character in a clear and positive way. For example, your story shows how you don't stop until the job is done. Or it can be impressive because others comment on how excellent your work was. It's great to hear stories where there are details like, "The CEO said she had never seen a proposal like that and asked me to create all of the future decks as well."

Go back to the document you created to jot down your Story Toolbox ideas and add three lines at the top, with the title "Top-Priority Stories." Then, reflect on your stories and choose your three strongest ones to copy there. These are going to be the three stories you will do your best to tell in most interviews. Next, rank each of your stories for the Story Toolbox to sit in the first or second spot under each prompt.

Ultimately, you'll notice yourself telling the same three

stories over and over in interviews, and that's okay—actually, that's fantastic! Your three top-priority stories will really hit on important points about the skills the company is looking for, and they will best show off your character. Not only will this ensure you are giving them the best peek into what it would be like to work with you, but these will also become your most practiced answers, so you'll become incredibly comfortable telling them each time they come up.

A final note: I often get the question "Can I repeat interview examples?" Never with the same person. But you can repeat stories at the same company. It is good practice to give different interviewers at a company different examples in case they compare notes, but never do that at the expense of giving a good answer. If two separate interviewers at the same company both ask you for a time you had to deal with a difficult customer, and you can only think of one example, don't fumble through a poorly improvised answer with the second interviewer. Stick with your tried-and-true example. (But that's also why I had you come up with two stories for every prompt, so you have quite the buffet to choose from!)

Practice for the Real Thing

Finally, it's time to practice your answers. It's stunning to me how few job seekers practice their interview answers out loud. If the first time you're saying your interview answer is in the interview, you are already setting yourself up for failure. Sure, you may be someone who is good "off the cuff," but imagine how much *better* you could have been had you put in a bit of preparation. The job offer is won by millimeters, so make sure you aren't cutting corners at any step of the way.

As you practice your answers, at first you can look down at your notes a couple of times to get your bearings, but you should lose that habit quickly as you practice. Go into your interview with just the titles of your stories. Each title should trigger your memory of the story, something like "Jr Dev mentor," and then you're on your own for sharing the CAR of it. I tell you to do this because while it's totally okay to have notes to reference in an interview, it's not okay to read off those notes as a script. It's best to hear the practice question, look down at your list of story titles, quickly choose one, fit the intro of the story to the question, walk through CAR, and then conclude by tying it all back to the initial question.

While speaking in front of a mirror is an excellent low-tech way of practicing, it's best to record a video of yourself and then watch the recording. This is a painful exercise, I know, but you'll be grateful for the insights you glean from seeing yourself from a new perspective. Suddenly you realize how much you say "um," touch your face, and seem to drift off midanswer. This allows you to make game-changing alterations to your interview approach.

Bringing It All Together

Your Story Toolbox is your ticket to making a lasting impact in your interviews. Stories are an incredibly powerful way to connect with potential employers on a deeper level and show clearly that you are the best candidate. Crafting your Story Toolbox involves brainstorming and prioritizing your stories, then practicing your responses, and using the CAR Method to convey your experiences with clarity and impact.

Your top stories should be impressive and align closely with the role you're seeking. Remember, you'll likely find yourself repeating these stories across interviews, and that's perfectly fine. Repetition builds confidence and ensures you consistently convey what it would be like to work with you. As you practice, don't forget to record yourself and watch the playback to fine-tune your delivery and presentation.

Embrace the magic of your Story Toolbox and the CAR Method and set yourself up for interview success. Your ability to share memorable stories that showcase your character and skills will undoubtedly set you on the path to being a Job Shopper and landing the offer. Don't underestimate the impact of these small but powerful changes—they can make all the difference in your next interview.

Show-Don't-Tell Projects

Now let's move on to the second part of becoming an irresistible candidate: what I call a "Show-Don't-Tell" project, or an "SDT" for short. In many of life's purchase decisions, we get to try something before we buy. Apps offer free trials. Yoga studios give a free sample class to new customers. Sommeliers offer a sip of wine before we commit to the bottle.

Yet hiring managers don't have this luxury when picking a new hire: they often make a huge decision based solely on the application and interview process. They usually don't get to experience what it would be like to work with you. So you have to show them.

It is becoming more common for companies to ask job candidates to complete a project or provide a work sample as part of the hiring process. However, even if they don't ask for this, do it anyway.

> *Providing work samples is your moment to vastly stand out from your competitors.*

My Show–Don't–Tell strategy has led to thousands of job offers, and it is where you don't wait for a company to ask you to do a project or provide work samples. Instead, you take the initiative.

If you are underqualified for the role, this unprompted additional step squashes many objections a hiring panel could have about your ability to perform the role and puts you firmly in the running for the offer. And if you are already well qualified, then adding a Show–Don't–Tell project isn't even fair—those other candidates don't stand a chance!

> *The truth is: no one does this strategy.*

In all my years of hiring, I can count on one hand how many people have implemented this strategy to land an interview or offer. One time, I even read a job description that encouraged candidates to include a project to show they were a fit for the role. When I asked the hiring manager how many people followed that tip for their application, he said zero. This is all to say that including a Show–Don't–Tell project is a dramatically underutilized strategy to help you stand out during the interview process.

There are three moments where you can bring in a project, whether encouraged by the company or not. You can first submit a Show-Don't-Tell to a company as a way to land an interview. This is especially advised if it's a competitive company to work for or you are an unconventional candidate who could use a boost to your application to show you've got the goods. Second, you can bring Show-Don't-Tells into the job interview to greatly elevate your answers with examples and visuals. And finally, you can submit a Show-Don't-Tell to the hiring manager in between interviews as a bit of a Hail Mary to land the next interview if you're not sure you'll get another one. (If you were already granted the next interview, then don't do this. Just wait until the next interview to have a chance to walk through the Show-Don't-Tell.)

Over the following sections, we will walk through how to craft an SDT. This includes how to figure out what kind of SDT to create, how to craft it, and then how to share it. Do note: the project and work samples you put together don't have to be "right." For example, if you are going for a marketing role and you identify the company's five best social posts and five lowest-performing social posts and come up with insights and recommendations based on that information, it doesn't have to be the "right" answer for why certain posts performed better or what will work, since you don't have access to their social account analytics for key data.

Additionally, the insights you provide may be things they already know, or things they can't act on for one reason or another. Who cares? This isn't about delivering them work that is at the same quality as someone on the team who has been working on it for weeks and has all the necessary context and resources. Instead, view this as a way to show the hiring manager how you think and problem-solve, and give them an idea of what it would be like to work with you.

If all this feels weird or uncomfortable, good. It's because you've likely never done this before, or seen someone do this. When you're a Job Shopper, you will do things that push your boundaries. Most people are scared to do anything beyond what a company directs them to do in an interview process and don't want to stand out in a bad way, so they don't take any calculated risks. This makes it incredibly easy to be the most compelling candidate of the bunch, because people are painfully predictable in their fear of messing up the job search process.

Determine the Focus of Your Show-Don't-Tell

Get out a document (I recommend a digital document, but a notebook works, too) and respond to each of the following four prompts to help you brainstorm what SDT you should create for your target opportunity.

1. LIST THE MOST IMPORTANT SKILLS / KNOWLEDGE / EXPERTISE FOR THE ROLE.

Good news: you already did this work when you walked through the GLORY Formula! So go ahead and hit copy-paste on the keywords you identified for this opportunity, and move right along to prompt number two.

UX Designer

**LIST THE MOST IMPORTANT SKILLS /
KNOWLEDGE / EXPERTISE FOR THE ROLE**

- user experience
- user interviews
- interaction flows
- wireframes
- visual design mock-ups

2. IDENTIFY CURRENT SKILL GAPS YOU HAVE FROM THE LIST ABOVE.

When coming up with a great SDT, one strategy can be to put together a work sample that squashes any objections the hiring team may have about your experience. So note any skill gaps you may have from the core skills list as a potential SDT focus.

EXAMPLE:

UX Designer

**IDENTIFY CURRENT SKILL GAPS YOU
HAVE FROM THE LIST ABOVE**

Haven't conducted user interviews.

3. LIST WORK YOU'VE DONE THAT SHOWS SKILLS RELEVANT TO THE ROLE.

If you don't have any skill gaps to address, the skills and experience you already have that are perfectly in line with the opportunity are what you'll want to showcase. You've already done the work, so why not make it easy on yourself and use that to show you've got what it takes?

In the case of our UX designer, you'll see they have lots of opportunities to show documentation of user journeys, wireframes, and mock-ups as work samples.

EXAMPLE:

UX Designer

LIST WORK YOU'VE DONE THAT SHOWS SKILLS RELEVANT TO THE ROLE

Created interaction flows to map out user journeys and identify pain points in a web application, focusing on streamlining the navigation process.

Developed wireframes for a new e-commerce platform, collaborating with cross-functional teams to ensure alignment with user needs and business goals.

Built visual design mock-ups for a responsive website, incorporating branding guidelines and usability principles to enhance aesthetic appeal and user engagement.

4. LIST WORK YOU COULD DO TO SHOW THE SKILLS RELEVANT TO THE ROLE.

This final prompt is where you'll brainstorm projects you can put together. You don't always have the perfect work sample ready and waiting, and it can be hugely impressive to put something together for the purpose of your interview. And quick reminder: Your work doesn't have to be fully accurate and actionable. Providing feedback on one customer support experience isn't exhaustive in an analysis, but again, it shows your initiative and the way you think.

For the UX designer example, since this person hasn't conducted user interviews, they can find users of the company they are interviewing with by asking friends and family or posting in online groups, and conduct user interviews with them. It's not official work, but the company is going to be very impressed that they took it upon themselves to talk to a few people and provide a short report with their insights.

EXAMPLE:

UX Designer

LIST WORK YOU COULD DO TO SHOW THE SKILLS RELEVANT TO THE ROLE

Conduct several user interviews of people who use the company's product and then share the findings.

Write a report about the user experience of two competitors of the company, and show how the company compares.

Design wireframes of a feature that the company's customers are asking for on forums.

Create It

Creating an SDT could take you as little as ten minutes or as long as ten hours. It really depends on what you're putting together. There are three buckets of SDT material that you should consider:

1. Visuals and Summaries
2. Work Samples
3. Custom Projects

The first two are fairly easy to put together, as these are based on work you've already done in the past. Custom projects, on the other hand, are done for the specific company you're interviewing for, and therefore will take more time and effort to assemble.

We will walk through each of these three types of SDTs. Depending on your profession, the company you're interviewing for, and, honestly, how badly you want the job, you'll likely mix and match these three strategies throughout your job search.

VISUALS AND SUMMARIES

You already have incredible accomplishments that are perfect for an SDT project. Take some of your notable work, whether paid, volunteer, personal, or academic, and summarize it.

What this looks like is taking screenshots of slides and documents, summarizing information in charts, or including photos as visuals, and then providing a high-level summary to go along with these items.

Many people make the mistake of sharing the entire presentation or project. No one has time to thoughtfully flip through your safety briefing presentation, so it's best to summarize the objective you were looking to achieve, the action you took, and the results pertaining to it (similar to the CAR Method).

Take some time to think about what key projects and initiatives you handled that show important skills related to the role you're interested in. For each of those accomplishments, consider: How can I show this visually?

Some ideas include:

- Photos from the event
- A high-level summary of a project
- Key quotes from clients, professors, coworkers, or customers
- Screenshots of several slides from a presentation, with a brief description to give context
- A summary of statistics in your role (number of calls taken, volume of inquiries managed, deal sizes, and so on)

Later in this chapter you will learn how to deliver this information, but spoiler alert: you should usually plan on using these items as visual aids when answering interview questions, instead of dumping a bunch of this information in the interviewer's inbox. I share this to urge you to not overstuff your SDT with information. Make it concise and easy to skim, and then allow your narrative skills to do more of the heavy lifting.

Consider now what visuals and summaries you could put in a document to utilize as visual aids when answering interview questions.

WORK SAMPLES

Now let's dive deeper into the deliverables of your past work. Our goal with providing work samples is so the interviewers can see for themselves our work quality. This is different from visuals and summaries, because those give high-level images and descriptions, whereas with work samples, the employer will see an email we sent, a spreadsheet we created, a website we designed—the focus is on walking through the actual work product.

You can imagine how powerful this is. The company's interviewers wonder if you're organized enough to manage their annual conference, and they might try to screen for this in an interview with a question like, "How do you stay organized?" Instead of rambling some intangible answer like the other candidates did, you pull up a beautifully color-coded and masterfully complex spreadsheet from a major event you coordinated. You blacked out sensitive information, such as people's names and contact information, but are able to walk through the thought process of how you designed the event and what you did to make it so darn organized. Work samples are excellent to show vivid representations of specific skills, which visuals and summaries may gloss over. The interviewer is certainly leaving that call convinced you can handle this role.

The process of putting together work samples is usually called having a portfolio, and it is common in creative careers like graphic design, product management, and marketing. But I challenge you to find ways to create your own portfolio even if you aren't in a creative field. Heck, I did this when I was interviewing for human resources jobs, so this can for sure work for your career, too! I shared work samples such as spreadsheets that showed the way I designed a compensation system for employees, job scorecards and other recruitment process tools, and documents of how I scoped out career succession planning in an organization. Over a decade after I did this in an interview, I ran into the CEO of that company. He told me I was one of the best hires he had ever made, and reflected on the time I pulled out my work samples in the interview, stating that was the moment he knew he was going to extend an offer to me. Talk about memorable!

Some ideas of work samples include:

- Emails sent to customers, clients, and email lists
- Screenshots (dashboards, interfaces, marketing materials, etc.)
- Spreadsheets (forecasting, planning, calculating, etc.)
- Presentations
- Agendas

These are only a few examples of the many ways you can show the work you have accomplished. Now that your mind has been opened to the world of work samples, in the future you'll be more diligent about collecting work samples at every place you work at, correct? Of course, don't post work samples with proprietary information on your public website, or create these SDTs on your work computer. Be discreet and you should be just fine.

CUSTOM PROJECTS

Building a custom project is the most impressive but also typically the most time-consuming approach of creating an SDT. This involves considering what is important to the business you're interviewing with, and then building a project that addresses that pain point. Custom projects are the best choice when you are facing a highly competitive talent pool (such as if you're interviewing with a well-known employer) and/or have some skill gaps or an unconventional background on your résumé.

For example, if you are going for a role in knowledge management, you could look for the lowest-rated articles in the company's help center and rewrite one of them to show how you'd improve it. Or you could create a report comparing the three top-rated help articles to the three lowest-rated, to identify trends and best practices. It's all about being creative!

If companies perceive you as having skills gaps, this is a great opportunity to squash those doubts. Let's say you're an elementary school teacher who is transitioning to be a digital marketer. Your marketing experience may be all freelance and project based—so the companies may question if you have "real" digital marketing experience. Make them eat those words by delivering a report where you share insights from surveying their audience on their impression of the business (or it could even be general sentiment in the industry), and present these insights to inform the digital marketing strategy the team could take for the holiday season.

The steps to uncover what custom project to take on for a company include:

- Review the job description and your notes from the interviews you've had with the company. What are the top focuses of this role?

- Pick one that could be used as a project or thought experiment.
- Write out the steps you'd need to take to complete the project. Revise the scope if it starts to feel out of reach.
- Begin working on it as soon as possible. If you're already in an interview process, time is especially of the essence.
- Submit it with your application, present it in the interview, or send it to the hiring manager midway through the interview process if they haven't yet granted you the next interview.

You may be sick of hearing me say this by now, but it bears repeating once more: Your insights don't need to be perfectly correct. Your survey doesn't have to be a randomized sample (it could be thirty of your friends and family members). You can make assumptions without the complete data you would have if you were actually in the company. This is because this project is showing your skills and initiative. You undoubtedly lack access to high-quality information and resources, and that is understood. What will shine through is how you are able to look at a challenge, break it down into steps, take action, and then show how you strategically think.

When you do share the materials, be sure to not be prescriptive to the organization. An attitude of "You don't have a mobile app, and your competitor does, so you need one" can feel a bit like you're telling them how to run their business. Instead, you should soften your language to something like, "A gap between you and the competitor that I found in my research is that they have a mobile app. This could be an area for growth for you if deemed necessary." Simply showing how you research and attack a challenge is more important than telling the company exactly what to do and how to do it.

Present It

Once your Show-Don't-Tell is complete, it's time to show that bad boy off. The best way to share an SDT is during the interview by integrating it into the conversation. Similar to what we saw with the 90-Day Plan, you'll be amazed at how easy it is to bring your SDT into the conversation when you have the objective in your head to make sure it's seen. If you have your visuals or work sample ready to go (let's say it's a production schedule you put together for an unscripted show), you could use it to answer tons of questions, such as:

What is your experience with unscripted television?
As a production manager, I [explain experience working on unscripted television].

I actually have an example of one of my production schedules here, would it be helpful to see it?

What is your biggest accomplishment?
My biggest accomplishment was [begin to explain a complex production that had tricky logistics, schedule, and budget].

I actually have the production schedule here—would it be all right if I share my screen as I tell you about this accomplishment?

[Tell full story while using the work sample as visual aid.]

Other questions where you could use this as an answer include:

- How do you stay organized when there are competing priorities?
- What is your approach to managing a production?
- What are some of your strengths?
- Tell me about your experience at _____ [employer].

You never want to force the work sample into the answer, but it can often be woven in flawlessly, and interviewers usually love it. Additionally, you likely have a collection of work samples, so you can pick and choose which ones to use based on the question asked.

I'm a firm believer that you can integrate custom projects into an interview even more easily than visuals or work samples. Let's take a look:

Why do you want this job?

Well, since interviewing with your company I have thought a lot about what it would be like to work here and the key challenges the team is facing. Which is why I put together [Custom Project]. May I walk you through it?

What's your experience in [skill]?

My experience is [give a bit of background], and I actually put that skill into action when preparing for this interview and created [Custom Project]. Do you mind if I share my screen to show you?

Other questions where you could use this as your answer include:

- Why should we hire you?
- Do you have any questions for me?
- How would you [related scenario]?

As long as your transition is smooth, and you don't appear to be dodging the question, this should be the greatest answer to their question that they've ever heard.

SHARING THE SHOW-DON'T-TELL BEFORE OR BETWEEN INTERVIEWS

As we discussed earlier in the chapter, there are times when you may share your SDT before landing the interview or between interviews. Submitting an SDT before the interview stage can be a potent way to stand out among an applicant pool. There are many different ways you can do this, and when choosing the best one, you should consider the context of your career path and quite simply what you think will work. One way to get your SDT to the hiring manager is to build relationships with people in the company, and then ask one of them to forward the SDT to the hiring manager. With a coworker sending them the email, the likelihood that they will open it goes way up.

You could also email it directly to the hiring manager, or I've even seen people email their project directly to the CEO. In your communications, explain the context of what you are sending them and express interest in working with the company. Be sure to follow up three times, after every three to five business days, because you'd be surprised how often hiring managers will respond on the third time and invite you for the interview. Another strategy is to post it on social media and then tag either the company or one of the executives.

As to submitting an SDT between interviews, this is typically done as an effort to solidify the next interview if you fear you may not land it. Possibly you left the last interview feeling like you didn't knock it out of the park, and the interviewer gave little indication that you would move on to the next round. At this point, you could wait in agony, or you could kick it into high gear and put together an SDT that hopefully will nudge the interviewers to give you another interview.

Do your best to send your SDT within a couple of days of the most recent interview. If you suspect that they may reject you, we want to get ahead of that before the shoe drops. Send it to the hiring manager with some context about what it is and reiterate your interest in the opportunity. You could even use screen share recording software to do a short video of you explaining the SDT, to simulate the experience of what it would be like in the interview. If you already have the next interview scheduled, or verbally confirmed that you'll have one, hold on to your SDT and share it during the interview.

So, to review:

- Bring a Show–Don't-Tell into the interview to stand out.
- If you're struggling to land the interview for a competitive role, create an SDT and share it with the hiring manager or others at the company.

- If you had an interview with a company and they haven't agreed to give you another interview yet, send an SDT to further persuade them.

Standing Out in the Interview

In order to make a splash in the interview process, you've now gathered two extraordinary tools that can put you on the path to success: the Story Toolbox, allowing you to transform any interview answer into an opportunity for the employer to picture you in the role, and Show-Don't-Tell (SDT) projects, which give employers a concrete look at how you work. With these tools, you'll be equipped to excel in job interviews, and you'll set yourself apart from the competition.

The Story Toolbox and SDT projects are your companions in showcasing your abilities, connecting on a deeper level with interviewers, and going beyond the norm in proving your worth. Embrace the power of storytelling and the audacity of taking calculated risks to set yourself apart in the interview process. When you don't give in to the fear of making the "wrong" move during an interview, you become a truly irresistible candidate.

Key Takeaways
- -
- **Craft your Story Toolbox by brainstorming and prioritizing stories that showcase your skills and experiences in the best light.**

- Use the CAR Method (Challenge, Action, Result) to flesh out your stories for behavioral interview questions, focusing on concise and impactful storytelling.

- Prioritize your top three stories based on relevance to the role and impressive accomplishments.

- Practice your interview answers out loud, focusing on delivering your stories confidently and naturally without relying on scripts or lengthy notes. Record yourself practicing and watch the playback to fine-tune your delivery, ensuring clarity and impact in conveying your experiences to potential employers.

- Create Show-Don't-Tell (SDT) projects and leverage them at key moments, such as to land interviews, or use them to enhance answers during interviews or secure next-round interviews by submitting them to hiring managers.

- Consider three types of SDT projects: visuals and summaries, work samples, and custom projects tailored to showcase skills and experiences.

Chapter 9

NEGOTIATION IS A PARTNERSHIP

Time and time again, my clients get *highballed* on their offers. Yes, highballed. Like Mona, who had been struggling to land the right job for over three years. She kept tweaking her résumé and applying to every relevant opening she could find, but no matter what she did, she couldn't attract the right kind of opportunity. At her wits' end, Mona invested in coaching and ultimately became a Job Shopper.

She went from three years of not seeing results, to landing an amazing role within just four weeks of getting coaching with my team.

Here's the spit-take moment: they paid her more than she was expecting—to the tune of $45,000 more than what she made in her last job, and $25,000 more than the posted salary amount on the job description.

How did she go from a candidate who was in low demand for three years to a candidate companies were stretching their budgets for?

It came down to two things:

1. She showed up as a Job Shopper for every step of the hiring process, causing the company to not want to lose her.
2. She followed the collaborative negotiation approach outlined in this chapter to continue building a relationship with the hiring manager, while pushing the salary to new heights.

When it comes to discussing salary, there are simple steps for maximizing your potential offer. But first, you have to see the negotiation as a chance for partnership, not battle.

I asked my audience online whether or not they had negotiated their most recent job offer. A staggering 42 percent said that they took the offer without negotiating. Unfortunately, I consistently see numbers like this when I ask this question. Many people don't negotiate their job offer, for several reasons. First, there is a fear that the company may take the offer away or that the candidate may appear ungrateful. Second, there's a bit of confusion as to what are the "rules." For example, if the salary range was posted online or discussed in the first interview, is there still a chance to discuss it when an offer is presented? Finally, if the person is happy with the offer they received, they're afraid to push for more if it could potentially sour the relationship.

While I understand these sentiments, I still encourage my clients to negotiate. There are two main reasons: One, the company expects you to negotiate. Often when an offer is created, there's a bit of wiggle room with the compensation to adjust it, even if it's at the top of the posted salary range. Two, if they extend an offer and you accept immediately with no discussion, they might think: "We overpaid for this person. We should have offered lower!" This sets the tone for you to get fewer or lower salary increases from the company in the future.

Of course, there are counterexamples where the company is explicit about the exact amount they're going to pay, and has a policy of not negotiating. Depending on the situation, in that scenario I might innocently ask at the offer stage, "Which aspects of this offer are negotiable, if any?" Either they will reinforce their stance or you will get some useful insider knowledge, such as, "We can't budge on the base salary due to our salary bands, but we could do a sign-on bonus or adjust your work-from-home days if that's valuable to you."

What you'll learn in this chapter is that it's not so much what you ask for but how you ask for it that will ensure the negotiation goes smoothly. Just as we wanted to get on the same side of the table as the interviewer during the interview, we now want to see the negotiation as another opportunity to build a lasting relationship with whoever we're negotiating with.

It is normal to fear that a negotiation could damage the relationship, and many job seekers worry that when the job market is highly competitive, they cannot negotiate. This is far from the truth, but the way you talk about money and salary could get you eliminated in a competitive job market if you are not careful. I'll help you find exactly the right words.

You will also come away knowing that if you negotiate and there isn't any change to the offer, it does not mean you failed. If anything, it should help you sleep at night knowing that you verified you received their top offer. Follow the steps laid out in this chapter closely and you may be shocked at the compensation increase you receive.

Navigating the "Salary Question" Early in the Process

You're barely a few minutes into your first interview with a company and they hit you with the "What is your expected salary?" question. Or worse, it's in the job application before you've even applied. It feels a bit like rushed intimacy—like being asked about your credit score on a first date.

> *The simplest advice I can give you: The first person who names a number loses. I want you to avoid giving a number if at all possible.*

I get so much pushback on this advice, with the main rebuttal being that you should just tell them what you're looking for so that you don't waste your time in the process. I completely understand this sentiment, and with this strategy there is a possibility that you could waste your time. But there's also a possibility that you could get far more money than you imagined.

I have been on the employer side of thousands of negotiations, and the candidates who wait until the end to negotiate on average get bigger increases to their offers. The reason is, when a hiring team determines you are the candidate they want to give an offer to, they are sold on you. They have fallen in love with how wonderful you are, and already have a photo of you in their wallet and a spot at the dinner table for Thanksgiving.

On top of that, they are exhausted from all the interviewing and just want the hiring process to be over. Therefore, you hold a lot of power in this moment. You have the power to make their dreams come true, and also make their nightmares end. Additionally, when you make asks in the negotiation, you're doing so from a position of the company better understanding your value. Whereas, if you come out guns a-blazing in the first interview with a high salary demand, they likely won't even take the time to get to know you because you're perceived as too expensive.

When companies ask for your target salary in a job application, well, this is another reason to avoid applying online, as we have talked about extensively. But if you're still filling out an application, you can write something like "flexible."

Some online applications have a drop-down menu where you have to select from a range of salaries, and you can't move forward without answering the question. In this case, your research on the role is important. We will talk more about research in this chapter, but it is important that you select a range that doesn't lowball you, but also isn't too high. When I worked in recruiting, I was instructed to eliminate candidates from consideration who put their range too high, simply for the reason that we couldn't afford them and didn't want to give them a disappointing offer. If you put too high of a range, but would have accepted a lower salary, I'd hate for you to miss out on opportunities you would have accepted.

Similarly, if you're asked about salary expectations during the first interview, you'll want to avoid giving a number. You don't want to say a number that is too high and eliminates you from consideration before the company fully understands your incredible value. Additionally, you don't want to say something too low, because once you say it, it's likely they will give you what was at the bottom of your range.

So when you are asked,

> *"What are your salary expectations?"*

say,

> *"I'm open. I am looking for the best fit and overall package."*

And isn't that the truth? There is so much more to a job than the salary—the projects, manager, flexible lifestyle, commute, and growth opportunities are all meaningful parts of the package. A good offer is more than a base salary, it's a combination of everything tangible and intangible that matters to you. So, going into this discussion, make sure you keep what you're shopping for in mind and know what you value most.

Unfortunately, some of these interviewers are going to be like an elevator: they won't budge until you give them a number. They may say, "Got it, sounds like you're flexible, but what range of compensation are you looking for?" At this point you'll dust off the old badminton racket and hit 'em back the birdie:

> *"Do you have a range that you're targeting so I can let you know if I'm comfortable with it?"*

If you're lucky, they'll tell you right then and there, easy-peasy. Other times, they will insist that you give them a number.

This is, again, when doing your research ahead of time pays off (literally). Before you get to the interview, you need to research how much the company pays for the job you're interviewing for, if that information isn't already on the job description. If there is not enough data there, research comparable companies: companies in the same industry, located in the same city, and of similar size. You can find an updated list of salary research sites at reversethesearch.com/resources.

You should aim for numbers higher in the range. I suggest making the bottom of your range somewhere between the 50th and 80th percentile of the ranges you're seeing online. And the top of your range should be aligned with the top of the range you found during your salary research. Employers usually give you the lowest number in your range, so you need to make sure the lowest number is one that you would be excited to accept.

Now, we have to acknowledge that salary research is very fuzzy. The validity of the salary ranges you see can be dubious at best. That's why I don't want you to get too technical about how you calculate this. Because salary research could also be you talking to people in your industry, asking them how much they've been paid and how much you should be expected to be paid. It's also the salary ranges you see on job descriptions, your current salary, as well as what other companies are offering you—these are all relevant data points. There isn't some magical range that you and the company will have landed on; it is a muddy process that you can use to your advantage *because* of its imprecision.

So if you are forced to answer the recruiter's insistent question, you can phrase your response carefully. Say something like,

> *"Before the call, I was looking at different salary ranges for types of companies like yours in your city for this type of role. What I was seeing was a range between $176,000 and $197,000. Does that fall in your range?"*

Make sure you don't draw a line in the sand that you can't back down from. The recruiter might say that $176,000 is their absolute max, and you can quickly pivot to say, "Depending on the other aspects of this role, I could see how that salary could be a piece of a great overall package."

Here is a review of the steps to take when discussing salary early in the hiring process:

- Avoid applying online and instead get your application submitted by referral so that you don't have to include salary range on the application.
- If you have to fill out a salary on an application, skip the question if possible or put a well-researched range.
- In the interview, respond to the salary question with, "I'm open; I am looking for the best fit and overall package."

- If they ask again, say, "Do you have a range that you're targeting so I can let you know if I'm comfortable with it?"
- If they still push for a number, say, "What I saw from similar companies hiring for this role was a range between \$_____ and \$_____. Does that fall in your range?"

Negotiating at the Offer Stage

MIT Human Dynamics Lab researchers Alex (Sandy) Pentland and Jared Curhan conducted a study where they used sociometers to analyze forty-six negotiations simulated by college students playing boss and employee.[*] They were measuring the social cues the participants were giving off, and ignoring the actual words being said. The task was to negotiate a new job offer, and the researchers found that the first five minutes of the sociometric data strongly predicted the outcome of the negotiation. Put another way, it was the rapport the negotiator built and the impression they made that allowed them to get a better deal in the end.

An important takeaway here is to remember that you'll possibly be working with these people as coworkers, so continue to build that relationship in the negotiation.

When I say that the negotiation should be a partnership, it can be clear as mud as to what that actually looks like in

---

[*] J. Curhan and A. Pentland, "Thin Slices of Negotiation: Predicting Outcomes from Conversational Dynamics within the First 5 Minutes," *Journal of Applied Psychology* 92 (2007), 802–11.

practice. While you will be edging for the best possible compensation, it can be done with tact and diplomacy.

Following are the three major elements to remember when you begin a negotiation.

1. Gratitude

Show gratitude for the initial offer and any adjustment to the offer, even if it's not exactly what you had hoped for. It's a strange feeling for the employer to choose you out of the other candidates and get excited for you to join the team, only for you to snap into "negotiation mode." So when you receive the offer, or different versions of the offer, always start by saying thank you and expressing your interest in the potential of working together, and then you can get down to business.

2. Clarification

Ask questions when appropriate to understand how they are crafting the offer, so that you can have mutual understanding. The questions can sound like these:

- "You mentioned that if we increase the salary by $10,000 that would put this role at the senior manager level. What skills and experience differentiate a manager from a senior manager employee?"
- "Regarding the performance-based bonuses mentioned in the offer, could you clarify how those are

structured and what criteria are used to determine eligibility?"

- "Can you provide more details about the equity component of the offer? Specifically, what type of equity is being offered (stock options? restricted stock units?) and what is the vesting schedule?"

So many job seekers don't even dream of asking these questions, but Job Shoppers do. That way they are discussing the opportunity with shared information and understanding, leading to a more open conversation and less potential resentment on either side.

3. Acknowledgment

Before you dive into your demands, acknowledge where the company is coming from, its limitations, and the accommodations it is making.

Practice active listening to the employer's concerns and perspectives, responding thoughtfully and empathetically. Be flexible and open to compromise, demonstrating adaptability and a willingness to work together toward a mutually beneficial outcome. For instance, if the employer expresses concerns about budget constraints, you could respond by acknowledging that perspective.

You might say something like, "I understand that the industry is hitting tough market conditions right now and budgets are tight, so I appreciate your effort to try to increase this offer. It means a lot." Statements like this suggest you're on the same team—you're not simply out to get the highest possible offer, but working together to execute a fair offer within the company's constraints.

◼

In these examples, practicing active listening, being flexible, and demonstrating a willingness to collaborate contribute to a constructive negotiation process where both parties can find common ground and work toward an outcome that benefits both.

Recognize that the negotiation is just the beginning of your relationship with the employer, so prioritize building a positive and respectful rapport. To stay calm and confident throughout the negotiation process, thorough preparation is essential. Research industry standards, company culture, and comparable salaries for your position to know your worth and be well-informed.

Negotiation Steps

When you receive a job offer, pause. Consider it. Even if it's the greatest offer you've ever heard, don't explode with enthusiasm at that moment. Take a beat, and then thank them for the offer. As mentioned, the first thing to do when receiving a job offer is to show gratitude. Even if it's a lowball offer, start with gratitude first:

> Thank you so much for this job offer. I have really enjoyed getting to know the team and I am excited at the possibility of working together.

Next, you can simply get the full details of the offer. Do not put pressure on yourself to negotiate in the moment if you're not a confident negotiator. It's okay to say that you want to take a moment to consider it and that you'll call them back. You can also ask for additional information if you haven't seen all the other aspects of the offer, such as the healthcare benefits, vacation, and other elements.

Then, after you've had time to think, or right away if you're feeling up for it, it's time to make the ask. You've done your salary research, you've spoken with other professionals in the field, and you've seen the pay ranges on other job descriptions and in interviews. Even if your offer comes in at market rate, challenge yourself to ask for more. Your ask can be as simple as this:

> Based on my conversations with companies and the salaries I am seeing in the market, I am targeting a salary of $_____. Is there a way to make up the difference?

A good practice also is to choose an unusual number. Instead of saying $155,000, for example, you might say $158,500. A Columbia University study found that precise numbers instead of rounded ones give the impression of having done deeper research.[*] I've also seen employers tend to meet in the

---

[*] Malia F. Mason, Alice J. Lee, Elizabeth A. Wiley, and Daniel R. Ames, "Precise Offers Are Potent Anchors: Conciliatory Counteroffers and Attributions of Knowledge in Negotiations," columbia.edu/~da358/publications/Precise_offers.pdf.

middle for negotiations, so by making "the middle" slightly higher, you may get a higher offer.

Be prepared in your negotiation to back up the salary amount you're asking for if necessary. This can be by stating the rate another company has offered you, sharing what you found in other research, or explaining why you deserve a salary at the higher part of their range due to your qualifications and unique expertise.

What typically happens is that the company won't go all the way up to the number you asked for. Instead, expect them to fall between their initial offer and what you said. That's why it is important to calculate the number midway between what they offered and what you asked for and make sure that is a number you would be happy with before you make the ask.

Another key point: in the name of Dolly Parton and all that is good, *please* stop talking.

> ### In negotiations, it's important to say less.

Too often I see job seekers ask for a certain salary, but then get nervous and backpedal, saying something to the effect of "But I understand that's a big ask, and there may not

$180,000 $190,000 $200,000

Company's offer — Negotiated offer likely in this range — Your target salary be flexibility." No! Stop talking. The rapport you built prior to making the ask should soften it enough to where you don't need to say things that weaken your position.

What to Negotiate for Besides Salary

If the company does not go all the way up to the salary you asked for, or perhaps doesn't budge at all, we still have lots of other things that you can negotiate for in the offer stage:

- **Your title.** The title could be higher or more specific, helping you gear up toward where you want to go next in your career.
- **A sign-on bonus.** A company is often more comfortable with giving you a bonus for signing the offer than it is with increasing your salary. That's because increasing your salary is a longer-term, more permanent change that could show pay inequity among positions, and sign-on bonuses are a way to get around that.
- **Severance.** Unfortunately, layoffs can happen. Ask during the offer negotiation whether your contract can include a predetermined amount of severance should your employment be terminated without cause. This is a great ask, because it gives you a bit of insurance but doesn't cost the company anything up front.
- **Stock options.** Depending on the company, you could ask for either more stock options or a shorter vesting period.
- **Office setup.** Your work environment can make a big difference, so ask for what matters to you, like an

office with a window, a standing desk, or an ergonomic chair.

- **A certain type of computer.** If you like a particular operating system or model, ask if that could be a possibility to eliminate your learning curve with a new technology.

- **Relocation assistance.** Typically, a company will set a maximum budget that is then reimbursement based, so you can send the company your receipts and they will directly deposit the amount into your account. It's a one-time cost for them and generally more palatable than a salary increase.

- **Flexible schedule.** You may want to work certain hours or work some days remotely. Whatever the case—discuss that in the offer stage.

- **Performance review.** If you didn't initially get the number you asked for as salary, ask if you can write a three- or six-month review into your contract to re-evaluate your compensation based on your performance. This allows you to prove yourself to the company, which both respects the risk the company is taking on you while expediting your timeline to land a raise.

Once you have discussed all the parts of the offer that are important to you, it's time to accept or decline the offer. My biggest advice here is to not overthink it. Accepting an offer should be easy and fun.

> *"Thank you for discussing the offer with me. I intend to sign, and I look forward to working together!"*

If you decline the offer, do so in a respectful manner. You don't need to give a reason, but if you do, I recommend giving a reason that is a bit out of their control. For example, let's say the reason you're declining is because you sensed the company doesn't value its employees (in more ways than one). Instead of saying that, you could share a secondary reason: "I really appreciate all the time you've dedicated to this process and for extending this offer. Unfortunately I'll have to decline. I would have been so fortunate to join your team, but it came down to choosing an opportunity where my commute was closer to my child's school."

There is nothing wrong with getting to the end of a hiring process and then saying no, and you'll have to get used to doing that as a Job Shopper. The best way to approach this is to be open-minded in the interview process, see opportunities through to the end, utilize the fact that you are in final rounds with a company to speed up other interview processes, and come out with multiple offers where you are making a thoughtful decision.

Secure the Best Overall Offer

As you prepare for your next negotiation, remember that salary negotiation is not a battle but a partnership. We are often afraid to negotiate, but if you approach it the right way, the conversation will continue to build the relationship, not break it. Building rapport and maintaining a positive relationship with the company throughout the process is crucial. When making your ask, it's not just about the number itself, but how you present it.

Additionally, it's not just about the money; it's about securing a package that aligns with your values and long-term career goals. You hold the power to shape your professional destiny. Each negotiation is a chance to assert your worth, shape your career path, and create a relationship built on mutual respect.

Key Takeaways

- When you earn a job offer, listen to the offer, pause, and then express gratitude and interest in potentially working together.

  "Thank you so much for this job offer. I have really enjoyed getting to know the team and I am excited at the possibility of working together."

- Don't feel pressured to give an answer in the moment. Ask additional questions about the offer, and even say you're going to process this information and get back to them promptly if you're not ready to talk numbers.

- When you do negotiate, be direct and succinct. State a target salary above what they are offering and see if they are open to raising their offer.

  "Based on my conversations with companies and the salaries I am seeing in the market, I am targeting a salary of $_____. Is there a way to make up the difference?"

- Don't speak after making that statement, and try to say as little as possible throughout.

- Depending on what they come back with for the offer, consider discussing salary further, or exploring other aspects of the offer to adjust.

- Accept or decline the offer with grace and appreciation.

Chapter 10

AIM FOR CAREER SECURITY

J ob security is a myth. Just ask my former client Albert, a dedicated senior manager who had invested sixteen years of his life at the same large, seemingly stable manufacturing company. When the business announced restructuring, Albert was aware that some people could lose their jobs, but was sure it couldn't be him. Lunches with the top executives, birthday parties surrounded by his colleagues, and his flawless work track record led him to believe that he could never lose his job—they simply wouldn't do that to him after everything they'd been through together.

But one day, Albert was summoned to a meeting room with the HR manager and his direct manager, who delivered the devastating news—he was part of the layoffs. Loyalty and dedication counted for nothing in the face of cost-cutting measures.

As he packed his belongings, Albert realized the stability he had believed in was an illusion. Leaving his employer that day, he carried the weight of betrayal and disbelief with him. The company he considered family had severed ties, and the once-secure future now appeared uncertain. Stepping into the unknown, Albert confronted the task of rebuilding not just his career but also his shattered sense of security.

Don't Depend on Job Security

The bottom line is, there's no such thing as job security anymore. Financial hardships hit, roles become redundant, and projects change. No matter how "loyal" you are, if a company hits poor financial times, they don't care if you gave the CEO your kidney, you're out of there.

And we often underestimate how many strong businesses fail. Once the largest international airline in the United States, Pan Am ceased operations after over sixty years commanding the skies. Toys R Us was a corporate juggernaut in the retail toy industry, operating hundreds of stores, only to close all of them in 2018. Groupon was once one of the hottest tech companies and had an initial public offering in 2011 that peaked around $30 a share, only to plummet the next year to below $4 a share.*

Nothing is a sure thing these days. Nonprofit organizations encounter funding challenges. Corporations lose market share.

---

* Wailin Wong, "Groupon Shares Fall on Weak Results," *Los Angeles Times*, November 10, 2012, https://www.pressreader.com/usa/los-angeles-times /20121110/281745561658159.

Government agencies have budget cuts. Additionally, a career you invest in today may not be here tomorrow. Being a travel agent used to be a popular career path, until travel websites largely squashed the need for a middleman. Journalist roles have been dropping precipitously in both compensation and number of job openings for decades due to the shift toward user-generated content. The need for bank tellers has sharply decreased as more people use ATMs and do their banking online.

While the profession you've dedicated your whole career to may not be going away completely, it's important to face the music when open roles in your path year over year are declining instead of increasing (as we discussed in chapter 3 when we learned about market demand).

As a Job Shopper, you accept that life isn't fair, and then manage whatever is actually in your control.

You don't chase job security; you seek Career Security.

Focus on Career Security

Job security is the idea that an employee's position within a company is stable and not at immediate risk of termination or layoff. Career Security, on the other hand, means that, should anything happen to an employee's job, they are positioned to swiftly get another.

Career Security means you have set yourself up to attract opportunities, so that if you lose your job, have to move cities for family reasons, or need higher cash flow, you'll have options to make an optimal career move. Instead of getting caught up in the devastating riptide of organizations' ebbs and flows, with Career Security you are ready to rumble should you ever need to hit the ejector switch on your current employment. That's powerful. And that's the life of a Job Shopper.

When Albert joined my coaching program after losing his job in the layoff, he hadn't searched for a job in over sixteen years. His online presence was minimal, his résumé was ancient, his knowledge of what skills were in demand was nonexistent, and his network was ice cold. Simply put, he did not have Career Security.

It took him a lot of effort to hit the restart button on his professional brand—from reengaging his past professional contacts, repositioning his experience to be marketable, and reacquainting himself with the key skills and knowledge he needed to be irresistible in the job market.

Albert ultimately landed a job in ninety days with a $40,000 salary increase at a company that was just a fifteen-minute commute from his home. He was thrilled, and he and his corgis lived happily ever after.

. . . Until he was laid off eighteen months later.

This would have been a run-out-into-the-rain-and-scream-at-the-sky moment, except Albert was surprisingly serene. All the hard work he had put into becoming a Job Shopper made it so that he didn't have to start from square one with this next job search. He already had recruiters regularly reaching out, his network was easy to reactivate, and he had gone into his most recent job tracking his achievements to prepare for future résumés and interviews.

His first offer came just three weeks after news of the lay-offs, and two more followed in the coming weeks. Albert ultimately chose a role that yet again gave him a salary increase and fit what he was looking for.

Being laid off was no longer a devastating hit to his finances, but instead an opportunity to propel his career forward. That is what Career Security can do for you.

Build Career Security in the Good Times

The worst thing you can do is stop flexing your Job Shopping muscles when things are going well. Just as we shouldn't go grocery shopping when we are hungry, it's also best to not start Job Shopping when desperate. You have steady income, you're not looking for a job, and you don't plan on making a career move in the near future—so now is the ideal time to build that security.

I have so many clients who tell me, "I wish I had been doing these things all along; that would make it so much easier now." Because it does. My clients say that their subsequent job searches are much easier, and they don't fear something going wrong anymore, because they are confident that they could land their next job if they needed to.

The only way you can guarantee your place in the market is by achieving Career Security. And the only way to achieve Career Security is by actively maintaining your Job Shopper status, in good times and in bad. By continuing to flex your Job Shopper muscles through the ups and downs of your career, you'll still have assets like your personal brand, marketable skills, and relationships, even if you were to lose your job tomorrow. These things never go away, as long as you take the time to build and sustain them.

Steps to Take to Achieve Career Security

Track Accomplishments

Remember all the agonizing work you put into the GLORY Formula? It'll never be that hard again, because once you've landed your new job, you are going to be tracking all your accomplishments. The first thing you want to do in your new role is take note of the current benchmarks. These are data points or the status of projects before you've gotten your hands on them. This could look like the number of employees currently at the company, the volume of traffic to the company's website, the state of the team's internal documentation. Make note of the "before" picture for anything you'll be working on. Not only will this help you to communicate in future job interviews about your contributions, but also it will be the perfect ammunition for asking for a raise or promotion.

We often forget a lot of the smaller projects or hard work we put into things, but by keeping a document that tracks all of it, you'll really start to see how much you actually contribute. For example, I took a look back at one of my accomplishments logs from a previous role and realized there were so many things that I'd forgotten about. One small detail that could be interesting in an interview answer is that I became responsible for the company's "all-hands" meetings, and a note I put next to this accomplishment was "I was the first person to ensure the meeting ended on time."

Memories flooded back of how these meetings tended to go fifteen and even thirty minutes over, prior to me being in charge. Just think about how disruptive that is! I was able to save every employee in the business thirty minutes each month. At the time, I took that accomplishment for granted, but, in hindsight, there's actually a lot of great detail I could expand upon in an interview if I wanted to discuss how I did it.

These are the important details that you will forget unless you actively maintain a log.

Build Relationships Internally

When you leave a company, you take away two invaluable things: the experience and the relationships. Many people don't intentionally focus on building meaningful relationships. Part of each workweek should be dedicated to grabbing coffee, in the break room or virtually, with people in the organization. It is best if there is a casual nature to it, where you are getting to know them on a deeper level rather than going over their comments on the most recent contract draft.

The people who somehow magically float to C-level status, potentially without being the shiniest penny in the jar, are doing this. And what is so brilliant about building relationships is that every single person you get to know who leaves the company becomes a potential referral at whatever company they work for next. This isn't about building relationships so that you get something from people, but it is important to realize that simply caring about people when you're in a company can almost ensure you are never unemployed.

I remember that, on the day I was laid off, word that 50 percent of the company's workforce had been eliminated made its way through the alumni of that company. I got texts from three different former coworkers insisting that I come to their workplaces to interview for head of human resources roles. They all told me that they had wanted to contact me sooner, but didn't want to disrespect our former employer and poach me from them. But now that I'd been laid off, reaching out to me was fair game. I suddenly felt incredibly secure in an insecure time, all because of the relationships I had built.

> *If you want Career Security, take a genuine interest in people.*

Fill your work calendar with fifteen-minute check-ins. For some people you'll talk every six weeks; for others it will be quarterly. It really depends on who it is. But your intentionality about keeping in contact with people will pay dividends. When I worked in an office, I would never miss a social event, even if I was tired; I would introduce myself if I noticed a new face; and I would eat my lunch in the busiest part of the office. Then when I worked remotely I would strike up one-on-one chat conversations with no objective every now and then, and I'd private-message people when we were in the same video meeting simply to say hi. These were low-lift ways to ensure I was building relationships with people seamlessly.

Get Clear on Your Next Career Step

One of the worst things you can do is wait until you get laid off or fired, or you are ready to leave your job, to finally ask yourself the question "What's next?"

You should be asking yourself, "What is my next career step?" consistently throughout your tenure at your job. The answer may be obvious, may change over time, or may be fuzzy, but do whatever you can to get clear with yourself. The reason this is so important is because the easiest way to become irresistible to the next employer and to land the exact opportunity you want next is to use your current employer to train you for that next opportunity.

Find job descriptions of what you'd like to do next. It could be what you're doing now, but with a higher title, or at a company with a bigger customer base. Look at the skill gap between where you are now and what that other role demands, and raise your hand for projects at your current company that could help build those skills (this can look like pushing to have more direct reports, asking to present in a board meeting, or getting on a project with global reach).

If you are looking to make any sort of career pivot, do your best to do most of the pivoting while still at the same company. It is much easier to pivot within a company than to leave and try to get another business to take a chance on your pivot. If you are working in product management, for example, but are interested in doing more employee training work, find ways that you can team up with the learning and development team, or do side projects that involve coaching or building learning experiences.

Many people believe heavily in the "law of attraction," which essentially is that when you get clear on exactly what you want, you can speak it into existence. It sounds a bit woo-woo, or too good to be true, but at the core, when you know exactly what you want, you notice opportunities that you wouldn't have seen otherwise. Also, people bring you opportunities because *they* are clear on what you're looking for. Good fortune seems to appear before you, but really the thing that opens doors is clarity and the ability to articulate what you want.

So settle into your next role and take a breath, but after a few months in, start asking yourself: "What do I want next? Do I want to do more of this, but at a higher level? Are there areas of the business or the profession that I would like to explore? Am I in the wrong place altogether?" Understand exactly what you want next, and then approach it like a Job Shopper, and I guarantee your career will move faster than it ever has before.

Keep Your Online Brand Up to Date and Your Network Warm

The trap that so many of us fall into is not updating our résumé or online presence until it is absolutely time to move on from our job. Instead of waiting too long, put a monthly event on your calendar, or every six or eight weeks if that feels like it comes up too quickly, and use that time to adjust anything that's outdated on your profile, add any new professional contacts to your LinkedIn network, and reach out to five people who you haven't talked to in a little while to see how they're doing.

You might be thinking that this sounds about as fun as getting an oil change or a flu shot—we know it's important to do, but we tend to put it off if we can. But once you are actually in motion, reaching out to people and updating what you've been up to, it really isn't so bad. As a matter of fact, you might even enjoy it. One of the biggest complaints job seekers have about networking is that it feels desperate or demanding, so imagine if you kept your network warm long before you were in the Job Shopping phase. Then if you need to ask them about their company or a job opportunity, it feels effortless and natural.

Additionally, one of the easiest ways to keep your network warm is to create content regularly on professional networking social media platforms, career-focused forums, or chat groups you're a part of, or to write blog posts. The reason this works so well is because you are networking at scale. You're reminding people that you exist and giving them an opportunity to comment if they care to. Then if you reach out to them to network or about an opportunity, it doesn't feel like you're contacting them out of the blue. These contacts have been seeing you online, and often welcome the conversation.

Become a Job Shopper at Your New Job

As we saw through Albert's story, after you have landed a fantastic new role, you have to be realistic about the fact that job security isn't real. You could invest years in a company, build relationships, and hone your skills only to discover that you've been laid off, effective immediately.

The ground beneath our professional feet is never as solid as it seems. Roles become obsolete, businesses face upheavals, and once-sturdy career paths morph into uncharted terrain.

So what's the antidote to this uncertainty? Becoming the Job Shopper you know you're capable of being. It's about ditching the rose-tinted glasses of job security and embracing a more pragmatic approach—Career Security. Forget about clinging to a job at a single company; focus on cultivating skills, nurturing professional relationships, and crafting a robust personal brand.

The essence of being a Job Shopper is clear: Be a wonderful employee at each place you work, but also understand that in the end, you're on your own, kid. No one else is looking out for your career; it's on you.

Career Security isn't a set-it-and-forget-it approach to your career; it's a lifelong commitment to staying relevant and resilient in the face of change. Because in the ups and downs of the job market, being a Job Shopper isn't a luxury; it's a strategic imperative. It's not about stumbling through the same dance routine; it's about mastering the dance steps even when the rhythm changes. So let's trade the illusory comfort of job security for the tangible strength of Career Security, turning the unpredictable job market into a canvas for ongoing success.

Key Takeaways

- Recognize that job security is a myth; shift your mindset to prioritizing Career Security, ensuring you're prepared for potential job loss or career transitions.

- Track accomplishments, cultivate meaningful relationships within your organization, clarify your next career steps, and actively pursue skills development aligned with your career goals.

- Regularly update your online presence and engage with professional contacts to maintain a warm network, making future job searches smoother. Consider creating content or participating in online discussions to expand your professional visibility and network.

Conclusion

Time and again, what I have found when educating people on becoming Job Shoppers is that I am dismantling years, and sometimes even decades, of beliefs around careers and success. Outdated ways of writing our résumés, ingrained habits that hurt more than help, and a fundamental misunderstanding of what are the actual "rules" of the job search, and when they should be broken.

If it has felt uncomfortable to implement what you've learned as you've followed along in this book, or if you're questioning if what this book teaches is even true, that is totally normal. We have been fed the wrong information for so long, told only how to follow what I like to call the "paved path."

The "paved path" claims that, if you obtain a level of education that is high enough, you won't have too much competition for the job you want and, as a result, you'll obtain a good salary. The "paved path" used to be as simple as getting an undergraduate degree, which would then lead to a great career. But once the paved path became the road often traveled, it became saturated. So what did people do next? They started getting MBAs and law degrees. Then that became saturated, and now people are going for PhDs at unprecedented rates, and still experiencing frustration at landing jobs, finding that they're overeducated and underqualified.

What I have presented to you in this book is the *unpaved* path. It looks more like a small trail off the main road that you might have passed by a few times, wondering if this is where the hike starts. For your whole career, this trail never had signposts—until now. If you trust the process of Job Shopping, even when it feels uncomfortable or as though you're seemingly going backward in your job search, I promise you, you will be setting yourself up for the best, and fastest, success with your career.

Through this book I hope you've realized that you have more pull in this game than you think. As companies compete for top talent, if you present yourself as a unique candidate in a league of your own, the organization will no longer see you as an interchangeable individual and will instead go above and beyond to get you on the team.

This all starts with knowing what you want. This is the part that so many professionals avoid, and it is actually one of the hardest questions to answer, but if you follow the steps laid out for you in chapter 3 to get clarity, you will ensure you're irresistible to companies. Knowing what you want allows you to put all your effort into fully immersing yourself in the industry and profession, attracting the right opportunities, and making businesses confident in bringing you on the team.

Once you know what you want, you must shed the terrible advice you've gotten about writing out your whole career history and what you find most interesting about yourself on your résumé and application. A Job Shopper realizes that their story isn't what the company actually values. Instead, companies just want to know if you can help them solve their problems. Look at what the job needs, learn about the company, and show how you are the solution to their challenges. This shift in and of itself will transform the way your résumé is received and how the interview feels.

Then you have to use every ounce of self-control you have to stop doing the same thing everyone does when looking for a job. *You need to move away from applying online.* It's a cattle call, and you should instead focus on being *found* online or getting a referral.

In this book I agonized about using the word "networking" since so many job seekers shut down and have major avoidance behaviors when hearing this word. It's ambiguous, feels inauthentic, and often reminds us that we are *not* nepobabies whose parents' rich friends have handed us jobs our whole lives. But while "networking" might sound like a buzzword, you need to shake the hesitation and fully embrace it as the strategy that will set you free. Networking is about building real connections. It's about noticing people, adding value, and weaving bonds that go beyond the usual small talk.

The interview is truly the most challenging part of the

process. While big actions land interviews, small actions land offers, so it's all in the nuance of embodying being a Job Shopper during every stage of the interview.

You'll want to metaphorically move your chair to the other side of the table. Focus on building rapport the same way you would if you already had the job and were simply meeting a coworker. Use the Consultative Approach to understand what this role will do and what might be sticking points, and begin considering how you would solve these problems. Put together a 90-Day Plan to show how closely you've been listening, and to allow them to further picture you in the role.

To spice up your interview even more, build out a Story Toolbox to provide answers that illustrate how you react to real-world situations, and create a Show-Don't-Tell project to get the interviewer tangibly seeing the way you work.

Finally, when it comes to talking about money, remember the old adage: whoever talks first, loses. Do your best to discuss compensation later in the process, when they can clearly see all your glory. Our goal is to get you in a league of your own, and they can't know that by simply looking at your baseball card. While some may view a negotiation as akin to a competitive tennis match, I instead recommend seeing it as rowing a boat together with the company representative; you're looking to find the right rowing rhythm so you can both make it to shore as swiftly and smoothly as possible. That said, don't forget to be bold in your negotiation. I encourage you to ask for a higher salary, and also explore other aspects of the offer that could enhance your position.

In the end, Job Shopping isn't about grabbing any old job; it's about nabbing the *right* one. It's about becoming the irresistible candidate that companies can't ignore. So, as you step into this adventure, remember to carve out your own path. Be vigilant and open, so that when the right opportunities come knocking, you'll be ready to swing the door open for them. With this foundation set and maintained, you'll have a career full of companies coming to you.

Job Shopping Doesn't End at the Job Offer

As you ride off into the sunset with your new employer, promise me one thing: you won't stop your Job Shopping ways.

> *Job Shopping is a mindset. An attitude. A lifestyle. It is not about having one foot out the door, but about always having a contingency plan in place.*

By following the advice in this book, you'll never feel forced to stay in any position, because you will have options. But as a Job Shopper, we don't use this fact as a threat. We value our current employment, we build relationships in a business, and we strive to do our absolute best work. We simply have a plan, know our value, and, as we're looking toward the next step in our career, always first go Job Shopping *within* the business we work in before looking outside the organization.

I'm not advocating for you to move from job to job quickly. In fact, there is immense value in spending years building a reputation and making a true impact on a business. Those relationships and accomplishments will only amplify your Job Shopping status more.

Instead, Job Shopping is about looking out for yourself, because in the end, no company will.

When you don't get the promotion, or you get laid off, or you suddenly need to relocate your whole life—no fairy job mother will appear. You control your own career destiny. You have to set yourself up for success.

Job Shoppers know what they want, speak up, and make power moves. They have fulfilling careers where they choose their employer each day. They don't give up when times get tough, but they also don't stay too long in a role that is eating away at their soul. They are secure in knowing their worth.

Why You're Not Actually Done with This Book

When I hear someone say that they read more than fifty books a year, I think that's a very positive thing. But for most of us, reading a large quantity of books should not be the goal. The goal should instead be to read a book, put the book's advice into practice, read it again, and continue to process its meaning, until we have mastered its contents. That's what I want you to do with this book. Read it every year. Keep yourself sharp.

I have clients who tell me that they have to listen to my advice over and over, both because the strategies are nuanced and take practice and because much of it runs counter to what we have been taught and are comfortable doing. Revisiting advice, even when we think we understand it intellectually, needs to happen for true behavior change.

Even better, once you start implementing the advice in this book and seeing the difference in your life, you can share what you have learned about Job Shopping with others. Not only will it be the single best way to solidify the teachings in your mind, but also you can change others' lives. We often want to help those we love with their careers, and one of the best things we can do in this situation is give them this book and allow them to steer their journey as they see fit. So much of my reach is built on people telling me, "My friend told me to follow you," or "My son recommended your strategies," and when incredible results start happening, those who were gifted Job Shopping advice are always so grateful to whoever sent them the resources.

The principles in this book are grounded in psychology. As long as humans are involved in the hiring process, these timeless principles will remain highly persuasive. (And honestly, so much of what is taught in this book would work on bots and algorithms, too—and already has.)

The stakes have never been higher. Old career advice is based on a less competitive landscape. But that's not what you're facing. You're facing a globalized workforce, with mass amounts of noise in the hiring process, and fast technology shifts that alter what skills are required, which jobs are in demand, and how companies hire.

As the job market gets more competitive, people often ask me: Can I still be a Job Shopper in a tough job market? My response is: That is the most important time to be a Job Shopper! Job Shoppers rise to the top of even the most crowded field of job openings. Job Shoppers evolve their skills to ensure they are always in demand over their lifetime.

The fast pace of technological and societal change makes these strategies more important than ever.

So make it happen for yourself! Kick rejection in the shins, throw fear in the trash, and send helplessness through the shredder. You're going to make this career move, and nothing will get in your way. You're a Job Shopper now.

Acknowledgments

The inspiration for this book came from a vast group of people who have supported and stood by me throughout my life. I have to first start by thanking my clients. I am so honored to be a part of your career journeys; thank you for trusting me. Your stories are the beating heart of this book and the reason I am excited to wake up Monday mornings and help others.

This book would not be possible without the incredible support of the team at 2 Market Media: Steve Carlis, Hank Norman, and Lauren Pringle. You all have pushed me to be a better version of myself ever since we met, and you three are nothing short of brilliant in what you do. Nena Madonia, you have coached me through every step of this journey, and have been my biggest advocate and an invaluable sounding board. To the team at Penguin Random House, it has been the greatest pleasure working with you! Megan McCormack, your edits made the book ten times better (I fear what I would be without you!), and you and Adrian Zackheim have been in my corner from the moment we joined forces.

Everything I do is possible because of the love of my wonderful family. My husband, Henry Elder, you make me feel invincible. I've made bold moves in my career that have felt scary at times, but I felt safe because you saw the greatness in me. And if no one thought what I did was good, I always knew I had one fan in you. You are the husband, father to our children, and life partner I've always dreamed of. Thank you for being the Christmas gift I cherish before a single present is opened. To my mother, Annette Benes Mann, who was probably more excited about my publishing this book than anyone. Your love has always been so deep, and has been the foundation that I have built my entire life on. To my father, Brian Mann, who has affectionately encouraged me to reach my potential at every stage of my life. I always look forward to your thoughts on the things I am building, and I can't wait to hear yours on this book. And to my brother, Michael Mann, thank you for always being there for me and being my first and longest best friend.

My mentors have played a huge role in building my career and the contents in this book. Chitra Ragavan—you are a powerful force of nature who is such an inspiration to me. Micah Winkelspecht—you gave me the greatest job of my life and the whole reason I started this coaching in the first place. Ellen Leggett—you encouraged me on this journey and have advocated for me time and time again; thank you to you and the USC Master of Applied Psychology Program. Liz Liu Anderson—I can draw a straight line from everything that my life became to your generosity and the example you set.

A huge reason I was able to write this book was the support of an incredible team. Courtney Copelin, Daphne Yu, and Shy Espinosa, thank you for the dedication you have had to supporting this mission of turning job seekers into Job Shoppers.

And finally, massive appreciation to everyone who has watched my videos, supported me online, and read this book. It's thrilling to be a small part of your life, and I wish the very best for you in your career!

Wi-fi high five!

Index

networks, networking, *(cont.)*
  laziest phrase in networking, 125
  LinkedIn and, 121, 128, 131, 135, 139
    (see also LinkedIn)
  mass networking, 108
  meeting new people, 130–31
    advocates versus avoiders and,
      133–34
    approach in, 132–33
    digital proximity and, 135–36
    finding the right people, 131–32
  misconceptions about, 114
  natural, 114–16
  negative attitudes about networking,
    113–19, 234
  online brand and, 100, 104–6, 113
  overthinking, 119
  recruiters and sourcers and, 94–104, 113
  referrals and, 113, 136–37, 234
  relationship building in, 114, 119,
    121, 122, 135
  60 Seconds of Value in, 117–18, 121,
    122, 124–26
    asking questions and listening,
      125–26
    brainstorming ideas, 129–30
    engaging in social media, 128
    extending invites to
      communities, 127
    making an introduction, 126–27
    sharing resources, 128–29
  size of network, 104–6
  timeline of networking calls, 118
  weak ties in, 111, 115–16
90-Day plan, 145, 158–63, 235
  reasons for creating, 158
  steps in creating, 159

Occupational Outlook Handbook, 51
offers, xv, xvii, 24, 111, 235
  accepting or declining, 215–16
  bonuses for, 214
  highball, 200–201
  negotiating, *see* negotiation
  90-Day plan and, 145, 158–63, 235
    reasons for creating, 158
    steps in creating, 159

  responding to, 211–12
  securing the best overall, 216–17
  taking without negotiating, 201
office setup, 214–15
Ong, Melissa, 12–14
online presence. *See* brand, online

Pan Am, 220
passions, 29, 34–37, 49
Pentland, Alex (Sandy), 208
performance reviews, 215
phone books, 93
privacy settings, 100–101

qualifications, 18–19. *See also* skills
  and aiming lower, 2–4
  degrees and certifications, 4–7
  job descriptions and, 17–18
    keywords and, 71
  percent of applications which meet,
    18–19
  recruiters and sourcers and, 94–104

rapport
  in interviews, 145, 146, 148–49, 235
  in negotiations, 211, 216
recruiters, sourcers, and headhunters,
  94–104, 113
referrals, 113, 136–37, 234
relationships
  negotiation and, 211, 216, 217
  networking and, 114, 119, 121,
    122, 135 *(see also* networks,
    networking)
  within companies, 225–26
relocation assistance, 215
resources, sharing, 128–29
responsibilities, accomplishments
  versus, 79–80, 85
résumés, xv, xviii, 7, 33, 61–92
  as about what you can do for the
    company, not about yourself, 62
  accomplishments on, 67, 79–85, 91
    action verbs and, 81, 83, 85
    keywords and, 81, 83, 85, 87, 91
    quantification of, 81–85
    responsibilities versus, 79–80, 85